THE OFFICIAL
MIXER'S MANUAL

Patrick Gavin Duffy

REVISED AND ENLARGED BY

Robert Jay Misch

SEVENTH EDITION

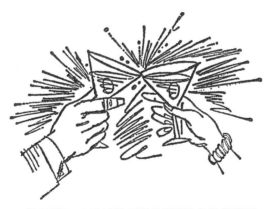

ILLUSTRATIONS BY REISIE LONETTE

1983

DOUBLEDAY & COMPANY, INC.

GARDEN CITY, NEW YORK

Library of Congress Cataloging in Publication Data

Duffy, Patrick Gavin.
  The official mixer's manual.

  Includes index.
  1. Liquors. 2. Cocktails. 3. Wine and wine making.
I. Misch, Robert Jay. II. Title.
TX951.D77   1983   641.8'74
ISBN: 0-385-18307-0
Library of Congress Catalog Card Number 82-45452

THE OFFICIAL MIXER'S MANUAL

CONTENTS

INTRODUCTION TO THE 1983 EDITION

I am proud to be identified with this, *The Official Mixer's Manual,* probably the most venerable and enduring book on alcoholic beverages on the bookstore shelves to this day. Beginning back in 1934, when drinking drinks and making them were barely legal, it has gone on its merry and helpful way. This is primarily due to the exhaustive compilation of the original author, with an able update from Jim Beard and—I like to think—my first update in 1975.

Let me give you an idea of why the need for a re-do. It's hard to believe, isn't it, that when good Pat Duffy first penned his pages, vodka per se was hardly known in these parts; it was something the Russians drank; tequila—well, who ever heard of *that?* Midori? Huh? Strega? Eh? Amaretto? What's that?

In those days, more mixed drinks were known and actually served than most bartenders today ever heard of or thought possible. BUT, they were compounded of far fewer basic ingredients. What I mean is that today gin makes primarily a Martini or a Gin and Tonic, but then, besides these drinks, with maraschino, it made a Seventh Heaven; with vermouth and pernod, it made a Some Moth; with vermouth and apple brandy, it made a So-So; and with a bit of Lillet and apricot brandy, it made the very "in" Charlie Lindbergh! In this book are over four hundred gin recipes alone, enough for a different one every day of the year with a lot left over.

Rye whiskey (and in the South, Bourbon) were the drinks of this country way back when. Today they are still our stars of the so-called brown goods. There are over seventy-five whiskey drinks in this book alone. These include drinks made with all the American whiskeys— Bourbon, American blends, rye.

Let me make that abidingly clear. Hear this: a number of years ago, I went out to the John F. Kennedy International Airport (then called Idlewild) to catch a plane. Said plane was reported an hour late, so I repaired to the bar and ordered a Scotch and Soda.

I was sipping away when I heard an unmistakable southern accent asking the bartender for an "Ol' Fitz 'n' Branch." I didn't look up. Suddenly the same voice boomed, "Watcha drinkin', son?" As I was the only "son" at the bar, the question had to be addressed to me. "Scotch and Soda," said I. The next thing I knew, a hand reached over, took my drink, held it over the counter and poured into the sink beyond. The voice again spoke to the bartender, "Give this young gen'leman an Ol' Fitz."

I looked up for the first time. He was a storybook, central-casting Kentucky colonel. His eyes twinkled so engagingly and his white moustache twitched so appealingly that I accepted the situation and said, "Well, thank you very much." We talked for perhaps half an hour—he really was from Kentucky, though not in the fried chicken business. Then we shook hands and parted, never to meet again. But I still have mental pictures of our man at the Kentucky Derby, walking about in the enclosure and tossing people's drinks onto the track, those that weren't "Ol' Fitz." In case you don't know, Old Fitzgerald is a very good Bourbon and still quite available.

DRINKS—WHAT AND WHERE

Eight years ago, when I wrote the introduction to the last revision of this *Manual,* I listed some thirty-two popular drinks in order of importance. The first ten represented 59 percent of all—and they still do, though the order has changed somewhat and the Daiquiri and Margarita would today make the first ten. Then, the first ten were:

> Gin Martini
> Manhattan
> Vodka Martini
> Scotch and Water
> Bloody Mary (with Vodka)
> Scotch
> Whiskey Sour
> Vodka (neat)
> Vodka and Tonic
> Canadian

Today the first ten are:

> Gin Martini
> Vodka Martini
> Manhattan
> Scotch (neat)/Scotch and Water
> Bloody Mary (all kinds)
> Daiquiri

Whiskey Sour
Vodka and Tonic
Vodka (neat)
Canadian Whisky
Margarita

Next time around, mark my words, Irish Coffee, Harvey Wall-banger, and various rum drinks will be edging up . . . up . . . up. What's happening is simply that the white goods have long overtaken the brown, and rum in its various guises has distanced the lot. Rum is the number one in spirits today. Of course, that means rum collectively: white, golden, dark; rum from Puerto Rico, Haiti, Barbados, Trinidad, Guyana, Jamaica, Martinique; and—yes—there's even a bit of good old New England rum still made.

Aside from rum, the greatest gains since 1975 in spirits (we'll get to wine in a separate section) have been scored by tequila and Irish whiskey. But remember, in percentage these are still a drop in the liter—but they're comers, along with the new "creams," Irish mostly but also some Italians. Vodka goes on and on, stealing customers from gin, and some even from whiskey.

WHERE DO WE STAND IN SPIRITS?

It might interest you to know that the consumption of spirits in the United States is far from first. The Woman's Christian Temperance Union and its allies, who brought us Prohibition (1917–33), know not what they wrought.

In fact, in consumption of hard liquor, we're eighth in the world. Poland is number one, downing four gallons per person per year. Who's second? Surprisingly, it's Luxembourg, with 3.8 gallons. Then come, in order, Hungary, East Germany, Czechoslovakia, Canada, and the U.S.S.R. And, finally, we make it—eighth internationally, with just a mite over two gallons per person per year.

GLOSSARY

Abricotine: One of the many French apricot liqueurs.

Advocaat: A brand of Dutch liqueur made of egg, brandy, and sugar, not unlike eggnog.

Alcool Blanc (White Alcohol): The colorless distillate (brandy) of fruit, berries, and roots, made in France, Germany, Switzerland, among other places. Kirsch (from cherries) is the best known; there are many others, including framboise (from raspberries) and fraise (from strawberries).

Amaretto: An immensely popular Italian almond-flavored liqueur.

Amer Picon: A popular brand of bitter cordial from France, with quinine and orange overtones—a favorite of the Foreign Legion.

Angostura Bitters: A brand of bitters from Trinidad.

Anisette: A sweet colorless liqueur with an anise flavor.

Apéritif: A drink of moderate alcoholic content, taken before meals, ostensibly to give one an appetite.

Applejack: The common name for apple brandy. Sometimes applies to the homemade product.

Aquavit (Akvavit): The national drink of the Scandinavians; caraway is basic though some other flavorings are sometimes used.

Armagnac: See BRANDY.

Arrack: See RAKI.

Bacardi: A brand of Puerto Rican rum.

Beer: A liquor, generally light-colored, fermented from cereals and malt, flavored with hops. Alcoholic strength about 6 percent.

Bénédictine: One of the oldest brands of the herb-flavored liqueurs of France. A Benedictine monk created the recipe which has remained a secret.

Berger: A brand of pastis of Marseilles.

Bitters: An infusion of aromatics, with bitterness the chief characteristic. The stronger bitters are used by the drop for flavoring; some popular brands: Angostura, Peychaud's, Herbsaint, Abbot's; also Boonekamp from Holland and Unicum from Hungary. Campari and Fernet Branca are brands of bitter apéritif wines from Italy.

Bourbon Whiskey: An American whiskey distilled from mash not less than 51 percent of which was corn grain. Must be aged in new barrels. May be a "blend" when mixed with neutral spirits or a "blend of straights" when blended with a number of Bourbons. "Sour mash" means that some of the previous day's slop, or leftovers, is used as today's starter.

Brandy: A spirit made from the distillation of wine or fermented fruit mash. Used alone, it refers to the distillate from grape wine only. *Cognac*—the special brandy distilled from the wine made from grapes grown in the Charente region, around the cities of Cognac and Jarnac, north of Bordeaux. *Armagnac*—the special brandy distilled in the Gers department, around the city of Condom in southern France.

Byrrh: A brand of reddish French apéritif wine, flavored with aromatics.

Calisayo: A Spanish liqueur with a bitterish aftertaste of quinine.

Calvados: An apple brandy distilled in Normandy.

Campari: A brand of popular Italian bitter apéritif wine, usually served with soda.

Canadian Whisky: A generic name for whisky produced in Canadian distilleries. Made primarily from corn. New cooperage not required.

Chambord: A brand of liqueur from Burgundy, made with black raspberries.

Chartreuse: This brand of French liqueur comes in two colors and strengths. Yellow Chartreuse is milder and lighter than the green. Both are made from a variety of herbs and aromatics and were originated by the Carthusians, a French order of monks.

CocoRibe: A brand of Virgin Island's Rum-coconut liqueur.

Cognac: See BRANDY.

Cointreau: A brand of orange liqueur made in France by the makers of Triple Sec, which it resembles.

Cordial Médoc: A brand of brandy liqueur from Bordeaux.

Crème de Bananes: A French banana-flavored liqueur.

Crème de Cacao: A dark brown liqueur from France made of cocoa beans, spices, and vanilla, with a brandy base.

Crème de Cassis: A dark red liqueur, or syrup, made from black currants. The basis of making a Kir.

Crème de Grand Marnier: A brand of rich liqueur from France, consisting of Grand Marnier and fresh sweet cream.

Crème de Menthe: A peppermint-flavored liqueur which comes in three colors: white, green or red.

Crème de Noyau: A French liqueur with a brandy base flavored with a variety of fruits and bitter almond.

Crème de Rose: A liqueur flavored with rose petals.

Crème de Vanille: A liqueur flavored with vanilla.

Crème de Violette: A lavender-colored liqueur, made from vanilla and cacao with a violet bouquet.

Crème Yvette: A brand of American liqueur similar to crème de violette but with a pronounced violet taste.

Curaçao: A liqueur made from the peel of Curaçao oranges which are grown on the West Indian island of Curaçao.

Cynar: An Italian apéritif made from artichokes.

Drambuie: A brand of liqueur made from Scotch whisky and honey.

Dubonnet: A brand of French apéritif wine made from aromatics. It has a slight quinine taste. Comes white (*blanc*) or red (*rouge*).

Falerum: A West Indian sweetener for rum drinks.

Fernet Branca: A popular brand of bitter apéritif wine from Italy, used as a stomachic.

Forbidden Fruit: A brand of American liqueur made from shaddock (a type of grapefruit), and cognac.

Fraise: A colorless brandy made from strawberries.

Framboise: A colorless French brandy made from raspberries.

Frangelico: A brand of Italian liqueur made from hazelnuts, herbs, and berries.

Galliano: A popular brand of Italian liqueur.

Gin: A liquor made with a neutral spirit base and flavored, generally, with juniper berries. Old Tom gin is a sweet gin. Holland gin has a heavy body and distinctive flavor and is usually drunk straight. American and British gins are dry and tight, except for individual brand flavorings.

Goldwasser: An orange-flavored liqueur of German origin, containing flecks of goldleaf. Usually called Danziger goldwasser, after the city of Danzig.

Grain Whisky: Spirits made from a mash of any cereal and/or corn, distilled at high proof, blended with malt whisky to make Scotch. Not unlike U.S. neutral spirits but usually aged.

Grand Marnier: A brand of orange-flavored French liqueur. Used widely in cookery.

Grappa: An Italian version of a marc, made from leftovers—skins, pits, etc.—of wine making.

Grenadine: A red, pomegranate-flavored syrup used for sweetening and color. Today the flavor is usually artificial.

Irish Cream: A relatively new Irish liqueur composed of Irish whiskey, sweet cream, and honey.

Irish Mist: A brand of liqueur based on Irish whiskey, herbs, and honey.

Irish Whiskey: A blend of malt whiskeys, some say the first whiskey in the world. Some Irish whiskey is blended these days with neutral spirits.

Izarra: A liqueur from the French Basque country, yellow and green, resembling Chartreuse. The green is the higher proof.

Kahlúa: A brand of coffee-flavored liqueur from Mexico.

Kirsch: A colorless brandy distilled from small black cherries.

Kümmel: A colorless liqueur, originally from Germany, with a caraway flavor.

Light Whiskey: A recent addition to the lexicon of American whiskeys. Distilled at a relatively high proof and usually blended with aged neutral spirits. Need not be aged in new cooperage, as with Bourbon.

Lillet: A brand of vermouth from Bordeaux, flavored with orange.

Liqueurs: Syrupy concoctions usually made by adding an infusion of fruits or herbs to grain alcohol, brandy, cognac, or whiskey. They are generally served after meals because of their sweetness, but also are frequently used as flavoring in cocktails or punches.

Lochan Ora: A brand of whisky liqueur made by the Chivas Scotch people.

Luxardo: A brand of Italian liqueur based on fresh maraschino cherries.

Malibu: A new American brand of liqueur made from rum, neutral spirits, and coconut.

Malt: Name given to sprouted barley, as used in making Scotch and Irish whisky. Malt whiskies give Scotch and Irish their distinctive flavors. In Scotland the four malt whiskies used in blending are based on geography: Lowland malts, Highland malts, Islays, and Campbeltowns. "Single malt" refers to any Scotch whisky that is bottled unblended from one individual malt whisky.

Mandarine: A brand of orange-flavored liqueur from France.

Maraschino: A strong sweet liqueur with a pronounced bittersweet cherry taste.

Marc: A strong French spirit distilled from pomace, the leftover grape skins, pits, and stems of wine making. Requires long aging. Marc de bourgogne and marc de champagne are the best known.

Midori: A brand of melon-flavored liqueur from Japan.

Mirabelle: A colorless Alsatian brandy made from yellow plums.

Monin: A brand of lime-flavored liqueur from France.

Ojén: An anisette from Spain.

Orange Bitters: A flavoring with a bittersweet orange taste used in cocktails and other drinks.

Orgeat: A flavoring syrup with a bittersweet almond taste.

Ouzo: A strong anise-flavor, unsweetened liqueur from Greece.

Panache: A brand of apéritif made in the United States.

Parfait Amour: A sweet, almondy, purple liqueur.

Pastis: A colloquial term used in France for anise-flavored liqueurs such as Pernod.

Pernod: The modern brand-name substitute in France for absinthe, which has been banned in most Western countries, because of the toxic effect of wormwood used in its manufacture. Pernod is anise-flavored and used as an apéritif and in many cocktails.

Pineau des Charentes: Apéritifs from the Charentes region of France, made from fresh grape juice and cognac.

Pisang Ambon: A banana-flavored liqueur made in Indonesia.

Porter: A very dark brown British beer with a bitter taste.

Proof: A measurement of alcoholic content. In the United States, the alcoholic content of a spirit is one half the indicated proof; thus, 100 proof indicates 50 percent alcohol. (The English use a somewhat different system; for example, their 70 proof is approximately U.S. 80 proof.) The alcohol in wine is measured by volume; 12 percent means 12 percent, not half as much, as in spirits.

Prunelle: A colorless French liqueur with the fragrance and flavor of plum.

Quinquina: An apéritif from France with a base of fortified wine and quinine. The word is sometimes used in referring to any apéritif wines.

Raki (Arrack, Arak): A rough anise-flavored spirit distilled variously in different countries: from grain in Greece; from dates in the Middle East; from palm sap and/or rice in South Asia; from sugar cane in Indonesia.

Ricard: A brand of pastis from Marseilles.

Rum: A liquor made from the fermentation and distillation of sugar cane. The color of rum has nothing to do with its alcoholic content.

Rye Whiskey: An American whiskey distilled from mash not less than 51 percent of which is rye grain.

Sabra: A brand of Israeli liqueur, orange-flavored, with a taste of chocolate.

St. Raphaël: A popular brand of apéritif wine from France.

Sake: A Japanese wine of 12-to-16 percent alcohol, made from a fermented rice mash. Colorless and sweetish; usually served warm.

Sambuca: A brand of anise-flavored liqueur from Italy.

Schnapps: A term from the German used in Middle Europe for any strong distilled liquor. Schnapps is often flavored.

Scotch Whisky: The whisky of Scotland, distilled from a mash of grain, primarily barley.

Slivovitz: A potent plum brandy from Yugoslavia and other Balkan countries.

Sloe Gin: A sweet liqueur made of gin and sloe berries.

Southern Comfort: A brand of American liqueur with a Bourbon whiskey base and a peach flavor, often used as a mixer.

Stone's Ginger Wine: A brand of English wine made of currants and flavored with ginger.

Stout: Strong, dark, heavy, bitter British beer.

Strega: A popular brand of orange-flavored liqueur from Italy.

Suze: A bitter French apéritif made from gentian.

Swedish Punsch: A pale yellowish liqueur with a slight rum flavor.

Tequila: A Mexican liquor distilled from mescal, or Mexican century plant, a cactus.

Tia Maria: A brand of coffee-flavored liqueur from Jamaica.

Tiddy: A brand of liqueur made from Canadian whisky.

Triple Sec: A brand of colorless liqueur from France, with a sweet orange flavor.

Tuaca: A brand of semisweet Italian liqueur from Leghorn, compounded of brandy (grappa), milk, and vanilla, with a butterscotch flavor.

Van der Hum: A brand of South African liqueur made from brandy and flavored with tangerines.

Vielle Cure: A brand of aromatic liqueur from Bordeaux, based on brandy and herbs.

Venetian Cream: An Italian cream-and-wine concoction not unlike the Irish creams.

Vermouth, Dry: A dry, aromatic apéritif wine, frequently used in cocktails.

Vermouth, Sweet: An aromatic apéritif wine, sweet and more highly flavored than the dry. Frequently used in cocktails.

Vodka: A spirit, native to Russia, Poland, and the Baltic states but now one of the fastest growing white spirits in the United States. The American version is nearly colorless, odorless, and tasteless. (Once a potato derivative, it is now mostly made from grain.)

Whiskey/Whisky: The generic name for liquor of not less than 80 proof (U.S.) that is distilled from a mash of grain. The American and Irish varieties are spelled *whiskey/whiskeys;* the Scotch and Canadian varieties, *whisky/whiskies;* for general references in this book, *whiskey/whiskeys* will be used. See Glossary for further details, under BOURBON WHISKEY, CANADIAN WHISKY, GRAIN WHISKIES, MALT, SCOTCH WHISKY, etc. (For more details, see headnote to section entitled "Cocktails—Whiskey Base.")

STANDARD LIQUOR MEASUREMENTS

A. STANDARD U.S. BAR MEASUREMENTS

Imperial (Imperiale)—approximately 8 bottles or 6 liters
Gallon—4 quarts, or 128 ounces, U.S.
        British imperial gallon is approximately 1.2
        U.S. gallons or 4½ liters.
Quart—32 ounces (English quart is 40 British fluid ounces).

1 quart	32 ounces
1 pint	16 ounces
⅘ quart (fifth)	25.6 ounces
1 wineglass (average)	4 ounces
1 jigger	1½ ounces
1 pony	1 ounce
1 teaspoon	⅛ ounce (approx.)
2 teaspoons	1 dessertspoon
3 teaspoons	1 tablespoon
1 cup	8 ounces
1 dash	1/32 ounce (approx.)

Some homely expressions, often used and meaning different things to different people:
    Splash—a generous spoonful.
    Dollop—a good-sized splash.
    Touch—just a few drops.
    3 fingers—about 3 ounces.

B. METRIC SIZES

By January 1, 1980, the entire U.S. liquor industry completed its conversion to the metric system. The tables below show the old sizes and the new ones (1 = liter; ml = milliliter).

For distilled spirits

Old U.S. package	U.S. ounces	New metric package	U.S. ounces
½ gallon	64.0	1.75 l	59.2
Quart	32.0	1.00 l	33.8
Fifth	25.6	750 ml	25.4
Pint	16.0	500 ml	16.9
½ pint	8.0	200 ml	6.8
Miniature	1.6	50 ml	1.7

For wine and champagne

U.S. term	Standard metric size	U.S. ounces
Magnum	1.5 l	50.7
Bottle	750 ml	25.4
Half bottle	375 ml	12.7
Split	187 ml	6.3

C. OTHER CHAMPAGNE BOTTLE SIZES

These are rarely seen today, but offer a challenge to a champagne-lover's imagination:

	Bottles
Jereboam	4
Rehoboam	6
Methuselah	8
Salmanazar	12
Balthazar	16
Nebuchadnezzar	20

PUNCH CUP

HIGHBALL GLASS

LARGE BRANDY SNIFTER

PILSNER GLASS

SMALL BRANDY SNIFTER

DELMONICO

BEER MUG

OLD FASHIONED GLASS

WHISKEY SOUR

LARGE BOWL
WINE GLASS

CHAMPAGNE FLUTE

LIQUEUR GLASS

POUSSE-CAFÉ GLASS

RHINE WINE GLASS

COCKTAIL GLASS

TOM and JERRY MUG

COPITA SHERRY GLASS

SHOT GLASS

SILVER JULEP MUG

THE OFFICIAL MIXER'S MANUAL

CHAMPAGNE—COCKTAILS AND PUNCHES

[Note: Because of the nature of this very special wine, all drinks using it as a base, regardless of their type, have been placed together in this section.]

Alfonso Cocktail
½ jigger Dubonnet
1 ice cube
1 dash bitters
1 lump sugar
Place the sugar in a large saucer champagne glass and sprinkle with bitters. Add ice and Dubonnet and fill with iced champagne. Serve with twist of lemon peel.

Barbotage of Champagne
Fill a tumbler ½ full of finely cracked ice. Add 1 dash of Angostura bitters, 1 teaspoon each of sugar syrup and lemon juice and fill with iced champagne. Stir lightly and serve with twist of orange peel.

Blue Train Cocktail (Champagne)
Shake well together, with cracked ice, ¼ brandy and ¼ lightly sweetened pineapple juice. Fill highball glass ½ full with this mixture and fill with iced champagne. (See Index.)

Champagne Cobbler
Fill a large goblet ⅔ full of cracked ice. Add ½ teaspoon lemon juice and ½ teaspoon curaçao. Stir and add 1 thin slice of orange and 1 small pineapple stick. Fill with iced champagne. Stir lightly again and serve with a straw.

Champagne Cocktail No. 1
Place 1 small lump sugar in a champagne glass and sprinkle with 1 small dash Angostura bitters. Add 1 small twist each or-

ange and lemon peel. Fill with iced champagne. Muddle gently.

Champagne Cocktail No. 2
Place ⅔ jigger Southern Comfort, 1 dash Angostura bitters, and 1 twist of lemon peel in a large saucer champagne glass. Fill with iced champagne.

Champagne Cooler
Place in a tall glass, ½ filled with ice, ⅔ jigger brandy, and ⅔ jigger Cointreau. Fill up with chilled champagne. Stir and garnish with mint.

Champagne Cup No. 1
(for 12–16)
Place in a punch bowl, with a block of ice, ½ pineapple cut in chunks, 6 good slivers of cucumber rind, 1 pint box of fresh strawberries, 3 jiggers curaçao, and 1 quart club soda. Stir lightly. Add 2 bottles iced champagne. Stir lightly again and serve.

Champagne Cup No. 2
(for 10–12)
Place in a punch bowl, with a block of ice, 2 tablespoons powdered sugar, 2 jiggers cognac, ½ jigger curaçao, ¼ jigger maraschino, ¼ jigger Grand Marnier, and 1 orange, sliced thin and seeded. Add 1 or 2 bottles iced champagne and decorate with pineapple, maraschino cherries, and fresh mint.

Champagne Fizz
Place the juice of 1 orange in a highball glass with several ice cubes. Fill with iced champagne.

Champagne Julep
Crush 4 sprigs mint with 1 lump of sugar and a few drops of water in bottom of your tallest highball glass. Half fill with cracked ice and add 1 jigger brandy. Fill with champagne and decorate with extra mint. Serve with straws.

Champagne Punch No. 1
(1 gallon)
Place in punch bowl ½ pound powdered sugar, 1 quart club soda, 2 jiggers brandy, 2 jiggers maraschino, 2 jiggers curaçao, and 3 jiggers lemon juice. Stir together and add block of ice. Pour in 3 bottles iced champagne. Decorate as desired.

Champagne Punch No. 2
(for 18)
Place in the order named in a large punch bowl, with a block ice, juice of 2 oranges, juice of 2 lemons, ½ cup sugar, ½ cup light rum, ½ cup dark rum, and 1 cup pineapple juice. Stir lightly and pour in 2 bottles iced champagne. Serve in punch glasses, decorated with fruit as desired.

Champagne Punch No. 3
(for 20)
Place 1 quart either lemon or orange ice in a punch bowl. Pour

over it 2 or 3 bottles iced champagne.

Champagne Punch No. 4
(for 15)
Place large block of ice in punch bowl. Add 2 jiggers brandy, 2 jiggers Cointreau, and 2 bottles iced champagne.

Champagne Punch No. 5
(for 10)
Place in punch bowl, with lots of ice, 1 jigger maraschino, 1 jigger yellow Chartreuse, 2 jiggers brandy, 1 pint club soda, 2 teaspoons sugar, and 1 bottle iced champagne.

Champagne Punch No. 6
(for 12)
Place in punch bowl 1 jigger brandy, 1 jigger curaçao, 1 jigger maraschino, 2 sliced seeded lemons, 2 sliced seeded oranges, and ½ basket strawberries or raspberries. Add 1 bottle iced club soda and 2 bottles iced champagne, or omit the club soda and add 3 bottles iced champagne. Place the punch bowl to chill in a bed of shaved ice and serve.

Champagne Punch No. 7
(Dragoon Punch) (for 20)
[Note: This punch is reputedly the cavalry man's answer to AR-TILLERY PUNCH; see Index.] Blend in a large punch bowl 3 pints porter, 3 pints ale, ½ pint brandy, ½ pint sherry, ½ pint sugar syrup, and 3 lemons, sliced

thin. Immediately before serving add a block of ice and 2 bottles iced champagne.

Champagne Punch No. 8
(individual)
Fill a large tumbler or highball glass ½ full of ice. Add the juice ½ lemon, ½ jigger framboise, 1 slice orange, and fill with iced champagne. Stir lightly and serve with straw.

Champagne Velvet (Black Velvet)
Half fill a tall glass with iced stout. Add iced champagne as desired. (Pour ingredients very slowly or glass will overflow.)

French 75
1 jigger dry gin
⅓ jigger lemon juice
1 teaspoon powdered sugar
Pour into tall glass ½ full of cracked ice and fill with chilled champagne.

French 95
Prepare same as FRENCH 75, using Bourbon whiskey instead of gin.

French 125
Prepare same as FRENCH 75, using brandy instead of gin.

I. B. F. Pick-Me-Up Cocktail
1 jigger brandy
3 dashes curaçao
3 dashes Fernet Branca
1 ice cube
Place in champagne glass and

fill with iced champagne. Squeeze lemon peel over top.

King's Peg
Place a piece of ice in a large wineglass. Pour in 1 jigger brandy and fill with iced champagne.

London Special
Place in a large highball glass 1 lump sugar, 1 large twist orange peel, 1 ice cube, and 2 dashes Peychaud's bitters. Muddle well and fill with iced champagne.

Mimosa
Place an ice cube in large wineglass. Add the juice of ½ orange. Fill with iced champagne.

Peach Bowl No. 1
Place in a large goblet 1 washed unpeeled perfect peach. Cover with iced champagne. Prick the peach several times to release the flavor and serve. (The peach, incidentally, is delicious eating after the drink is finished.)

Peach Bowl No. 2
This is prepared same as PEACH BOWL No. 1, but with a brandied peach and a little of the syrup. And you don't need to prick the peach to get the flavor!

Prince of Wales
Place in a shaker 1 dash Angostura bitters, 1 teaspoon curaçao, and ½ jigger each madeira and brandy. Shake well with ice and strain into a large wineglass. Fill with iced champagne and serve with a thin slice of orange.

Queen's Peg
Place an ice cube in a large wineglass. Add ½ jigger dry gin and fill with iced champagne.

Soyer-au-Champagne Cocktail
Place in a large saucer champagne glass 1 large teaspoon vanilla ice cream, 2 dashes maraschino, 2 dashes curaçao, and 2 dashes brandy. Stir together gently. Fill with iced champagne and decorate with a slice of orange and a cherry.

COBBLERS

BASIC COBBLER
The cobbler, which like the julep is a drink of American origin, is generally served in a large goblet. Fill ⅔ full of shaved or finely cracked ice. Sprinkle with 1 teaspoon fine granulated sugar, if desired, and pour in 1 or 2 jiggers claret, port, Rhine wine, sauterne, or sherry; or, if preferred, 1 or 2 jiggers applejack, brandy, gin, rum, whiskey, or vodka. Whatever is used, the glass should be decorated with a slice of orange and a small pineapple stick. Frequently mint is used.

Brandy Cobbler
Fill a tumbler ¾ full of cracked ice. Add 1 teaspoon curaçao, ½ teaspoon sugar, 1 or 2 jiggers brandy. Decorate with fruit.

Champagne Cobbler (see Champagne)

Claret Cobbler
Fill a tumbler ½ full of cracked ice. Add 1 dash maraschino, 1 teaspoon each sugar and lemon juice. Fill with claret and stir. Decorate with fruit.

Port Cobbler
Fill a tumbler ⅔ full of cracked ice. Add 1 teaspoon each orange juice and curaçao. Fill with port wine. Decorate with fruit. A very little sugar may be added if desired.

Rhine Wine Cobbler
Fill a tumbler ½ full of cracked ice. Add 1 teaspoon each sugar and lemon juice. Stir lightly and fill with Rhine wine. Decorate with twist of lemon peel and mint.

Sauterne Cobbler
Prepare same as RHINE WINE COBBLER, using sauterne instead of Rhine wine and omitting sugar and mint.

Sherry Cobbler
Fill a tumbler ⅔ full of cracked ice. Add a teaspoon each sugar and orange juice. Fill with sherry, stir slightly, and decorate with fruit.

COCKTAILS—APÉRITIF AND WINE BASES

AMER PICON

Picon
½ Amer Picon
½ dry vermouth
Stir well with ice and strain into glass.

Picon Grenadine
1 jigger Amer Picon
½ jigger grenadine
Place with ice cubes in old-fashioned glass and fill with club soda.

AQUAVIT

Danish Clam
In bottom of mixing glass shake a little salt, pepper and cayenne; ½ teaspoon Worcestershire; 1 teaspoon lemon juice; 2 jiggers aquavit; 1 jigger clam juice; 1 jigger tomato juice. Chill and serve.

BYRRH

Byrrh
⅓ Byrrh
⅓ rye whiskey
⅓ dry vermouth
Stir well with ice and strain into glass.

Byrrh Cassis
⅔ Byrrh
⅓ crème de cassis
Place in large wineglass with ice cubes and fill with club soda.

Byrrh on the Boulevard
Place 2 oz. Byrrh, with or without ice, in a large wineglass (or tall glass). Fill with club soda.

Byrrh Special
½ Byrrh
½ Old Tom gin
Stir well with ice and strain into small wineglass.

CAMPARI

[Note: There is also a cordial Campari. Do not confuse them; they are not at all alike. The cordial is an afterdinner liqueur made from fresh raspberries. Use it straight or with cut-up fruits over ice cream, in puddings, etc.]

Americano
1½ oz. Campari
1½ oz. sweet vermouth
Pour into cocktail glass. Stir with cracked ice. Add lemon twist.

Campari and . . .
Campari with soda or tonic, 3 to 1, is a favorite apéritif the world over. Use large wineglass.

Cranparie
2 oz. Campari
2½ oz. cranberry juice
Pour into cocktail glass. Stir with cracked ice. Add lemon twist for garnish.

Negroni
1½ oz. Campari
1 oz. gin
1 oz. sweet vermouth
Pour into cocktail glass. Stir with cracked ice.

DUBONNET

[Note: Dubonnet now comes both white and traditional red. These drinks use the red. The white is good for milder or less flavorful drinks.]

Appetizer
1 jigger Dubonnet
Juice of ½ orange
Shake well with ice and strain into glass.

Bob Danby
1 jigger Dubonnet
½ jigger brandy
Stir well with ice and strain into glass.

Manhattan (Dubonnet)
½ Dubonnet
½ whiskey
Stir well with ice and serve with a cherry. (See Index.)

Mary Garden
½ Dubonnet
½ dry vermouth
Stir well with ice and strain into cocktail glass. When served with a twist of lemon peel, this is called a MERRY WIDOW.

On-the-Rocks
Place twist of lemon peel and ice in old-fashioned glass. Then fill with Dubonnet.

Sanctuary
½ Dubonnet
¼ Amer Picon
¼ Cointreau
Stir well with ice and strain into glass.

Upstairs
2 jiggers Dubonnet
Juice of ¼ lemon

Pour into large cocktail glass
with ice cubes and fill with club
soda.

Weep No More
⅓ Dubonnet
⅓ brandy
⅓ lime juice
1 dash maraschino
Stir well with ice and strain into
glass.

FERNET BRANCA

Yodel
½ Fernet Branca
½ orange juice
Place ice cube in glass and combine ingredients. Fill with club
soda.

LILLET

Burnt Orange
Slice off bits of orange rind
about 1 inch long. Pour out a
glass of chilled Lillet. Take a bit
of rind in one hand. Light a
match with the other. Quickly
bend rind outward and touch
match to it. It will *pf-ff-ff* as the
exuded orange oil ignites. Plunge
rind at once into Lillet. (This
takes a little practice.) Stir and
serve.

Roy Howard
½ Lillet
¼ brandy
¼ orange juice
2 dashes grenadine
Shake well with ice and strain
into glass.

PANACHE

Chandon Judy
4 oz. Panache
2 oz. sparkling wine
1 dash bitters
Pour Panache and bitters into a
champagne flute and fill up with
chilled wine.

Panache Negroni
1½ oz. Panache
1 oz. Campari
1 oz. dry gin
Shake well with ice and strain
into cocktail glass.

PERNOD

[Note: All drinks that call for
absinthe may be made with
Pernod.]

Brunelle
¼ Pernod
¾ lemon juice
1½ teaspoons sugar
Shake well with ice and strain
into glass.

Button Hook
¼ Pernod
¼ apricot brandy
¼ brandy
¼ white crème de menthe
Shake well with ice and strain
into glass.

Duchess
⅓ Pernod
⅓ dry vermouth

⅓ sweet vermouth
Shake well with ice and strain
into glass.

Frappé (Pernod)
1 jigger Pernod
⅓ jigger anisette
2 dashes Angostura bitters
Shake well with shaved ice and
strain into glass.

Glad Eye
⅔ Pernod
⅓ peppermint schnapps
Shake well with ice and strain
into glass.

Macaroni
⅓ Pernod
⅓ sweet vermouth
Shake well with ice and strain
into cocktail glass.

Nine-Pack
⅓ Pernod
⅓ curaçao
⅓ brandy
1 egg yolk
Shake well with ice and strain
into glass.

Nineteen-Pick-Me-Up
⅔ Pernod
⅓ dry gin
1 dash Angostura bitters
1 dash orange bitters
1 dash sugar syrup
Shake well with ice and strain
into glass. Add dash of club
soda.

Pansy
1 jigger Pernod
6 dashes grenadine
2 dashes Angostura bitters
Shake well with ice and strain
into glass.

Pernod
¾ Pernod
¼ water
1 dash sugar syrup
1 dash Angostura bitters
Shake well with ice and strain
into small highball glass.

Pernod Colada
1½ oz. Pernod
1 oz. colada mix
1 tablespoon pineapple juice
Mix with crushed ice and strain
into cocktail glass. Garnish with
a chunk of pineapple.

Pernod Sunrise
1½ oz. Pernod
1 oz. Cointreau
1 oz. grenadine
1 oz. orange juice
Mix well with crushed ice and
strain into cocktail glass.

Screwdriver (Pernod)
2 oz. Pernod
4 oz. orange juice
Mix well with crushed ice and
strain into cocktail glass. (See
Index.)

Suisse
1 jigger Pernod
4 dashes anisette
1 egg white
Shake well with ice and strain

into glass. Sugar syrup may be used in place of anisette.

Victory
½ Pernod
½ grenadine
Shake well with ice and strain into glass. Fill with club soda.

PINEAU DES CHARENTES

Black Tie
2 oz. Pineau des Charentes
1 oz. sparkling white wine
Mix and serve with ice in wine-glass.

French Tonique
2 oz. Pineau des Charentes
2 oz. club soda or tonic
Mix and serve with ice in wine-glass.

Le Reynac
2 oz. Pineau des Charentes
1 oz. lemon juice
½ teaspoon sugar
Mix well and strain into cocktail glass over ice.

Le Sauvage
2 oz. Pineau des Charentes
1 oz. Cognac
Mix and serve on the rocks in a brandy glass.

PORT

Broken Spur
⅔ white port
⅙ dry gin
⅙ sweet vermouth

1 egg yolk
1 teaspoon anisette
Shake well with ice and strain into glass.

Chocolate (Port)
¾ port
¼ yellow Chartreuse
1 egg yolk
1 teaspoon crushed chocolate
Shake well with ice and strain into glass. (See Index.)

Devil's
½ port
½ dry vermouth
2 dashes lemon juice
Stir well with ice and strain into glass.

Port No. 1
2 jiggers port
1 dash brandy
Stir well with ice and strain into glass. Squeeze orange peel over top.

Port No. 2
2 jiggers port
2 dashes curaçao
1 dash orange bitters
1 dash Angostura bitters
Stir well with ice and strain into glass.

Port Sangaree
2 jiggers port
1 jigger water
½ teaspoon powdered sugar
Stir well with ice and strain into glass.

ST. RAPHAËL

Orange St. Raphaël
2 oz. St. Raphaël
2½ oz. orange juice
Shake well with ice and strain
into glass.

St. Raphaël Esprit
2 oz. St. Raphaël
1 oz. vodka
Stir with ice and strain into glass.
Garnish with lemon twist.

SHERRY

Adonis
⅔ dry sherry
⅓ sweet vermouth
1 dash orange bitters
Stir well with ice and strain into
glass.

Bamboo
½ cream sherry
½ sweet vermouth
1 dash Angostura bitters
Stir well with ice and strain into
glass.

Bomb (for 6)
6 jiggers cream sherry
1 jigger Cointreau
1 jigger orange juice
1 dash orange bitters
Shake well with shaved ice and
serve with an olive.

Brazil
½ dry sherry
½ dry vermouth
1 dash Pernod

1 dash Angostura bitters
Stir well with ice and strain into
glass. Squeeze lemon peel over
top.

Byculla
¼ sweet sherry
¼ port
¼ curaçao
¼ ginger ale
Stir well with ice and strain into
glass.

Coronation (Sherry)
½ sweet sherry
½ dry vermouth
1 dash maraschino
2 dashes orange bitters
Stir well with ice and strain into
glass. (See Index.)

Cupid
2 jiggers sweet sherry
1 egg
1 teaspoon powdered sugar
1 pinch cayenne pepper
Shake well with ice and strain
into glass.

Duke of Marlborough
½ sweet sherry
½ sweet vermouth
3 dashes raspberry syrup
Juice of 1 lime
Shake well with ice and strain
into glass.

East Indian
½ dry sherry
½ dry vermouth
1 dash orange bitters
Stir well with ice and strain into
glass.

Greenbriar

⅔ dry sherry
⅓ dry vermouth
1 dash peach bitters
1 sprig fresh mint
Shake well with ice and strain into glass.

Philomel

⅓ dry sherry
⅙ rum
¼ quinquina
¼ orange juice
1 pinch black pepper
Shake well with ice and strain into glass.

Pineapple (for 6)

Soak 1 cup crushed pineapple in 4 jiggers dry white wine for 2 hours. Add 2 jiggers fresh pineapple juice, the juice of ¼ lemon, and 6 jiggers dry sherry. Chill the shaker thoroughly but do not put any ice in the mixture. Stir when cold and strain into glasses. Serve with a small wedge of pineapple in each.

Plain Sherry

2 jiggers sweet or dry sherry
2 dashes maraschino
2 dashes Pernod
Shake well with ice and strain into glass.

Reform

⅔ dry sherry
⅓ dry vermouth
1 dash orange bitters
Stir well with ice and strain into glass. Serve with a cherry.

Sherry

2 jiggers dry sherry
4 dashes dry vermouth
4 dashes orange bitters
Stir well with ice and strain into glass.

Sherry and Egg

Carefully break 1 egg into a cocktail glass, leaving the yolk intact. Fill the glass with sweet sherry.

Sherry Twist No. 1 (for 6)

6 jiggers dry sherry
2 jiggers dry vermouth
2 jiggers brandy
1½ jiggers Cointreau
½ jigger lemon juice
1 small piece of cinnamon
Shake well with ice and strain into glasses.

Sherry Twist No. 2 (for 6)

5 jiggers sweet sherry
4 jiggers whiskey
1 jigger Cointreau
Juice of 1 orange
Juice of ¼ lemon
2 cloves
1 pinch cayenne pepper
Shake well with ice and strain into glasses.

Ship

½ sweet sherry
⅛ whiskey
2 dashes rum
2 dashes prune syrup
2 dashes orange bitters
Shake well with ice and strain into glass. A little sugar may be added if desired.

Straight Law
⅔ dry sherry
⅓ dry gin
Stir well with ice and strain into glass. A twist of lemon peel may be added.

Tuxedo
2 jiggers sweet sherry
½ jigger anisette
2 dashes maraschino
1 dash Peychaud's bitters
Stir well with ice and strain into glass.

Xeres
2 jiggers sweet sherry
1 dash peach bitters
1 dash orange bitters
Stir well with ice and strain into glass.

SWEDISH PUNSCH

Afterdinner Special
1 jigger Swedish punsch
½ jigger cherry brandy
Juice of ½ lime
Shake well with ice and strain into glass.

Doctor
1 jigger Swedish punsch
Juice of 1 lime
Stir well with ice and strain into glass.

Grand Slam
½ Swedish punsch
¼ sweet vermouth
¼ dry vermouth

Stir well with ice and strain into glass.

Hesitation
¾ Swedish punsch
¼ rye whiskey
1 dash lemon juice
Stir well with ice and strain into glass.

Hundred Percent
⅔ Swedish punsch
⅙ lemon juice
⅙ orange juice
2 dashes grenadine
Stir well with ice and strain into glass.

Margaret Duffy
⅔ Swedish punsch
⅓ brandy
2 dashes bitters
Stir well with ice and strain into glass.

Waldorf No. 1
½ Swedish punsch
¼ dry gin
¼ lemon or lime juice
Stir well with ice and strain into glass. (See Index.)

VERMOUTH

Addington
½ sweet vermouth
½ dry vermouth
Stir well with ice and strain into large cocktail glass. Fill with club soda and serve with twist of lemon peel.

Alice Mine

¼ dry vermouth
4 dashes sweet vermouth
½ Grand Marnier
¼ dry gin
1 dash Angostura bitters
Stir well with ice and strain into glass.

Bonsoni

⅔ sweet vermouth
⅓ Fernet Branca
Stir well with ice and strain into glass.

Cherry Mixture

½ sweet vermouth
½ dry vermouth
1 dash maraschino
1 dash Angostura bitters
Stir well with ice and strain into glass. Serve with a cherry.

Chrysanthemum

½ dry vermouth
½ Bénédictine
3 dashes Pernod
Stir well with ice and strain into glass. Serve with twist of orange peel.

Cinzano

2 jiggers sweet vermouth
2 dashes orange bitters
2 dashes Angostura bitters
Stir well with ice and strain into glass. Squeeze orange peel over top.

Crystal Bronx

½ dry vermouth
½ sweet vermouth
Juice of ¼ orange
Pour into large cocktail glass with ice and fill with club soda.

Diplomat

⅔ dry vermouth
⅓ sweet vermouth
1 dash maraschino
Stir well with ice and strain into glass. Add a cherry and squeeze lemon peel over top.

Fig Leaf

1 jigger sweet vermouth
⅔ jigger light rum
Juice of ½ lime
1 dash Angostura bitters
Shake well with ice and strain into glass.

Green Room

⅔ dry vermouth
⅓ brandy
2 dashes curaçao
Stir well with ice and strain.

Harvard Wine

⅔ jigger dry vermouth
½ jigger brandy
1 dash orange bitters
Stir well with ice and strain into large cocktail glass and fill up with club soda.

Humpty Dumpty

⅔ dry vermouth
⅓ maraschino
Stir well with ice and strain into glass.

Italian

⅔ sweet vermouth
⅓ Fernet Branca

2 dashes sugar syrup
1 dash Pernod
Stir well with ice and strain into
glass.

Nineteen
⅔ dry vermouth
⅙ dry gin
⅙ kirsch
1 dash Pernod
4 dashes sugar syrup
Stir well with ice and strain into
glass.

Pantomime
1 jigger dry vermouth
1 egg white
1 dash grenadine
1 dash orgeat syrup
Shake well with ice and strain
into glass.

Perfect
1 jigger dry vermouth
1 jigger sweet vermouth
1 jigger dry gin
Stir well with ice and strain into
glass. Serve with twist of lemon
peel.

Perpetual
½ sweet vermouth
½ dry vermouth
4 dashes Crème Yvette
2 dashes crème de cacao
Stir well with ice and strain into
glass.

Plain Vermouth (for 6)
10 jiggers dry vermouth
1 teaspoon Pernod
1 teaspoon maraschino
Stir well with ice and strain into

glasses. Serve with a cherry in
each.

Queen Elizabeth Wine
⅔ jigger dry vermouth
⅓ jigger Bénédictine
⅓ lime or lemon juice
Stir well with ice and strain into
glass. (See Index.)

Raymond Hitchcocktail
2 jiggers sweet vermouth
1 slice pineapple
Juice of ½ orange
1 dash orange bitters
Stir well with ice and strain into
glass.

Soul Kiss No. 1
⅓ dry vermouth
⅓ sweet vermouth
⅙ Dubonnet
⅙ orange juice
Stir well with ice and strain into
glass. (See Index.)

Spion Kop
½ dry vermouth
½ Dubonnet
Stir well with ice and strain into
glass.

Third Rail (Vermouth)
1 jigger dry vermouth
1 dash curaçao
1 dash crème de menthe
Stir well with ice and strain into
glass. Serve with twist of lemon
peel. (See Index.)

Trocadero
½ dry vermouth
½ sweet vermouth

1 dash grenadine
1 dash orange bitters
Stir well with ice and strain into glass. Add a cherry and squeeze lemon peel over top.

Tropical
⅓ dry vermouth
⅓ maraschino
⅓ crème de cacao
1 dash orange bitters
1 dash Angostura bitters
Stir well with ice and strain into glass.

Vermouth Apéritif
Place cracked ice in a cocktail glass. Fill with sweet vermouth and serve with twist of lemon peel.

Vermouth No. 1
2 jiggers vermouth (dry or sweet)
2 dashes Angostura bitters
Stir well with ice and strain into glass.

Vermouth No. 2
1½ jiggers sweet vermouth
½ teaspoon curaçao
1 teaspoon Amer Picon
½ teaspoon powdered sugar
1 dash Angostura bitters
Stir well with ice and strain into glass. Serve with twist of lemon peel and a cherry.

Vermouth Cassis (Pompier)
2 jiggers dry vermouth
⅔ jigger crème de cassis
Place in glass with ice cubes and fill with club soda.

Vermouth Frappé
1½ jiggers sweet vermouth
1 dash Angostura bitters
Stir with shaved ice and strain into glass.

Vermouth-on-the-Rocks
Fill old-fashioned glass with ice. Pour in sweet vermouth and serve with twist of lemon peel.

Washington
⅔ dry vermouth
⅓ brandy
2 dashes sugar syrup
2 dashes Angostura bitters
Stir well with ice and strain into glass.

Wyoming Swing
½ sweet vermouth
½ dry vermouth
1 teaspoon powdered sugar
Juice of ¼ orange
Shake well with ice and strain into glass.

York Special
¾ dry vermouth
¼ maraschino
4 dashes orange bitters
Stir well with ice and strain into glass.

WINE

Kir
Any dry white table wine, chilled, with a dash of crème de cassis.

Queer Kir
Chilled red wine
Dollop of Amer Picon
Stir well with ice and pour into glass.

STONE'S GINGER WINE

Ginger Snap
1 oz. Stone's ginger wine
3 oz. vodka

Stir in tall glass with crushed ice.
Fill with club soda.

Rum and Stone's
1½ oz. Stone's ginger wine
1½ oz. white or golden rum
Mix in glass with ice.

Whisky Mac
2 oz. Stone's ginger wine
2 oz. Scotch whisky
Mix in cocktail glass with crushed ice.

COCKTAILS—BRANDY BASE

[Note: Cognac, armagnac, grappa, calvados, apple brandy, etc., may be substituted for brandy.]

Alexander (Brandy)
⅓ brandy
⅓ crème de cacao
⅓ cream
Shake well with ice and strain into glass. (See Index.)

American Beauty
⅓ brandy
⅓ dry vermouth
⅓ orange juice
1 dash white crème de menthe
1 dash grenadine
Shake well with ice and strain into glass. Top carefully with a little port.

Aunt Jemima
⅓ brandy
⅓ crème de cacao
⅓ Bénédictine

Pour ingredients carefully into a liqueur glass so that they are in separate layers. Serve after dinner. Any liqueurs may be "layered" if you remember to use the heaviest bodied first, and so on to the lightest.

B. and B.
½ brandy
½ Bénédictine
Serve in a liqueur glass or iced in a cocktail glass. This is an after-dinner drink.

Baltimore Bracer
½ brandy
½ anisette
1 egg white
Shake well with ice and strain into glass.

Barney Barnato
½ brandy
½ Dubonnet

1 dash Angostura bitters
1 dash curaçao
Stir well with ice and strain into glass.

Betsy Ross
1 jigger brandy
1 jigger port
2 dashes Angostura bitters
1 dash curaçao
Stir well with ice and strain into a large cocktail glass. As an eye-opener this may be made with the yolk of 1 egg and 1 teaspoon of sugar. Shake with ice and strain into glass and serve with a grating of nutmeg.

Between-the-Sheets
⅓ brandy
⅓ Cointreau
⅓ light rum
Shake well with ice and strain into glass.

Block and Fall
⅓ brandy
⅓ Cointreau
⅙ calvados or apple brandy
⅙ Pernod
Shake well with ice and strain into glass.

Bombay (Brandy)
½ brandy
¼ sweet vermouth
¼ dry vermouth
2 dashes curaçao
1 dash Pernod
Stir well with ice and strain into glass. (See Index.)

Bomber
1 jigger brandy
⅓ jigger Cointreau
⅓ jigger anisette
⅔ jigger vodka
Shake well with ice.

Bonnie Prince Charles
1 jigger brandy
½ jigger Drambuie or Lochan Ora
Juice ½ lime
Shake with ice cubes.

Booster
2 jiggers brandy
4 dashes curaçao
1 egg white
Shake well with ice and strain into glass. Serve with a grating of nutmeg.

Bosom Caresser
⅔ brandy
⅓ curaçao
1 teaspoon grenadine
1 egg yolk
Shake well with ice and strain into glass.

Brandy
2 jiggers brandy
½ jigger curaçao
1 dash Angostura bitters
Stir well with ice and strain into glass. Serve with twist of lemon peel.

Brandy Blazer
2 jiggers brandy
1 small twist orange peel
1 twist lemon peel
1 lump sugar

Place sugar in bottom of shaker and add other ingredients. Stir with a long spoon; blaze for a few seconds and extinguish. Strain into glass. Serve after dinner.

Brandy Champarelle
1 jigger brandy
½ jigger curaçao
½ jigger yellow Chartreuse
½ jigger anisette
Shake well with ice.

Brandy Flip
1 jigger brandy
1 whole egg
1 teaspoon sugar
2 teaspoons cream (optional)
Shake with ice cubes. Dust with nutmeg.

Brandy Gump
2 jiggers brandy
2 dashes grenadine
Juice of ½ lemon
Shake well with ice and strain into glass.

Brandy Sour
1½ jiggers brandy
Juice of ½ lemon
1 teaspoon sugar
Shake well with ice and strain and serve in a Delmonico glass. Add a cherry and, if you want, a twist of lemon peel.

Brandy Special
2 jiggers brandy
2 dashes curaçao
2 dashes sugar syrup
2 dashes bitters

1 twist of lemon peel
Stir with ice and strain into glass.

Brandy Vermouth
¾ brandy
¼ sweet vermouth
1 dash Angostura bitters
Stir well with ice and strain into glass.

Builder-Upper
1 jigger brandy
⅔ jigger Bénédictine
Juice of 1 lemon
Shake well with ice cubes in tall glass. Fill with club soda.

Cecil Pick-Me-Up
2 jiggers brandy
1 teaspoon sugar
1 egg yolk
Shake well with ice, strain into large cocktail glass and fill with iced champagne.

Ceylon
1 jigger brandy
½ jigger dry vermouth
⅓ jigger Triple Sec
½ jigger dry sherry
Juice of ½ lemon
1 stick of cinnamon, broken (or 1 shake ground cinnamon)
Shake well with ice and strain into glass.

Champs Élysées
1 jigger cognac or brandy
½ jigger Chartreuse
½ jigger lemon juice
⅓ tablespoon powdered sugar
1 dash Angostura bitters
Shake well with ice and strain into glass.

Charles
½ brandy
½ sweet vermouth
1 dash Angostura or orange bitters
Stir well with ice and strain into glass.

Cherry Blossom
1 jigger brandy
1 jigger cherry brandy
⅓ tablespoon curaçao
½ tablespoon lemon juice
⅓ tablespoon grenadine
Shake thoroughly with shaved ice and strain into glass.

Chicago
1 jigger brandy
1 dash curaçao
1 dash Angostura bitters or Pernod
Stir well with ice and strain into glass frosted with sugar. Fill with iced champagne.

City Slicker
⅔ brandy
⅓ curaçao
1 dash Pernod
Shake well with ice and strain into glass.

Classic
½ brandy
⅙ curaçao
⅙ maraschino
⅙ lemon juice
Stir well with ice and strain into glass frosted with sugar. Squeeze lemon peel over top.

Coffee No. 1
⅓ brandy
⅓ Cointreau
⅓ cold black coffee
Shake well with ice and strain into glass. May be served after dinner.

Coffee No. 2
⅔ brandy
⅓ port
2 dashes curaçao
2 dashes sugar syrup
1 egg yolk
Shake well with ice and strain into small glass. Serve with a grating of nutmeg. (This cocktail has no coffee in it but if properly made it should be coffee colored.)

Cold Deck
½ brandy
¼ sweet vermouth
¼ white crème de menthe
Stir well with ice and strain into glass.

Coronation (Brandy)
⅔ brandy
⅓ curaçao
1 dash peach bitters
1 dash white crème de menthe
Stir well with ice and strain into glass. (See Index.)

Corpse Reviver No. 1
½ brandy
¼ calvados or apple brandy
¼ sweet vermouth
Stir well with ice and strain into glass. (See Index.)

Cuban No. 3
⅔ brandy
⅓ apricot brandy
Juice of ½ lemon
Stir well with ice and strain into
glass. (See Index.)

Davis
⅔ brandy
⅓ dry vermouth
4 dashes grenadine
1 dash Angostura bitters
Stir well with ice and strain into
glass.

Deauville
¼ brandy
¼ calvados or apple brandy
¼ Cointreau
¼ lemon juice
Stir well with ice and strain into
glass.

Depth Charge
1 jigger brandy
1 jigger calvados or apple
brandy
½ teaspoon grenadine
½ tablespoon lemon juice
Shake gently with ice and strain
into glass.

Devil
⅔ jigger brandy
⅔ jigger green crème de menthe
1 pinch red pepper
Shake brandy and crème de
menthe and strain into glass.
Sprinkle red pepper on top.

Don't Go Near the Water
½ brandy
⅙ curaçao

⅙ maraschino
⅙ lemon juice
Shake well with ice and strain
into glass frosted with sugar.
Serve with twist of lemon peel.

Double Trouble
⅔ brandy
⅓ dry vermouth
4 dashes grenadine
1 dash Angostura bitters
Shake well with ice and strain
into glass.

Dream
⅔ brandy
⅓ curaçao
1 dash Pernod
Stir well with ice and strain into
glass.

East India
¾ brandy
⅛ pineapple juice
⅛ curaçao
1 dash Angostura bitters
Stir well with ice and strain into
glass.

Egg Sour
1 jigger brandy
1 jigger curaçao
Juice of ½ lemon
1 egg
1 teaspoon sugar
Shake well with ice and strain
into Delmonico glass.

Fancy
2 jiggers brandy
Dash Angostura bitters
Frost rim of glass with lemon
and sugar. Shake ingredients

thoroughly with ice. Strain into glass and fill with iced champagne.

Flying Fortress
1 jigger brandy
⅓ jigger Cointreau
⅓ jigger anisette
⅔ jigger vodka
Shake well with ice and strain into a large glass.

France
2 oz. cognac
1 oz. Grand Marnier
1 oz. lemon juice
Shake with ice and strain into glass.

Frank Sullivan
¼ brandy
¼ Cointreau
¼ Lillet
¼ lemon juice
Shake well with ice and strain into glass.

Froupe
½ brandy
½ sweet vermouth
1 teaspoon Bénédictine
Stir well with ice and strain into glass.

Gazette
½ brandy
½ sweet vermouth
1 teaspoon lemon juice
1 teaspoon sugar syrup
Stir well with ice and strain into glass.

Grenadier
⅔ brandy
⅓ ginger brandy
1 dash jamaica ginger
1 teaspoon powdered sugar
Stir well with ice and strain into glass.

Harry's Pick-Me-Up
2 jiggers brandy
1 teaspoon grenadine
Juice of ½ lemon
Shake well with ice and strain into glass. Fill with iced champagne.

Harvard
½ brandy
½ sweet vermouth
2 dashes Angostura bitters
1 dash sugar syrup
Stir well with ice and strain into glass.

Hoop La
¼ brandy
¼ lemon juice
¼ Cointreau
¼ Lillet
Stir well with ice and strain into glass.

Horse's Neck (Brandy)
Prepare same as HORSE'S NECK (WHISKEY) using brandy instead of whiskey. (See Index.)

Ichbien
¾ brandy
¼ curaçao
1 egg yolk
Milk as desired.
Shake well with ice and strain

into glass. Sprinkle with nutmeg.
Excellent for the morning after.

Lady Be Good
½ brandy
¼ white crème de menthe
¼ sweet vermouth
Shake with cracked ice and
strain into glass.

Let's Slide (Poop Deck)
½ brandy
¼ port
¼ blackberry brandy
Shake well with ice and strain
into glass.

Loud Speaker
1½ oz. brandy
1½ oz. gin
½ oz. Cointreau
½ oz. lemon juice
Stir well with ice and strain into
large cocktail glass.

Lugger
½ brandy
½ calvados or apple brandy
1 dash apricot brandy
Stir with ice and strain into glass.
Serve with twist of orange peel.

Mabel Tea
1 jigger brandy
⅓ jigger Amer Picon
Juice of ½ lime
Shake well with ice and strain
into glass.

Metropolitan
½ brandy
½ sweet vermouth
2 dashes sugar syrup

1 dash Angostura bitters
Stir well with ice and strain into
glass.

Mikado
1 jigger brandy
2 dashes curaçao
2 dashes orgeat
2 dashes crème de noyau
2 dashes Angostura bitters
Stir well with ice and strain into
glass.

Mrs. Solomon
1 jigger brandy
2 dashes curaçao
2 dashes Angostura or orange
bitters
Stir with ice and strain into glass
frosted with sugar. Serve with
twist of lemon peel.

Morning
½ brandy
½ dry vermouth
2 dashes Pernod
2 dashes maraschino
2 dashes curaçao
2 dashes orange bitters
Stir well with ice and strain into
glass. Squeeze lemon peel over
top and serve with a cherry.

Newton's Special
¾ brandy
¼ Cointreau
1 dash Angostura bitters
Stir well with ice and strain into
glass.

Nick's Own
½ brandy
½ sweet vermouth

1 dash Angostura bitters
1 dash Pernod
Stir well with ice and strain into
glass. Squeeze lemon peel over
top and serve with a cherry.

Night Cap
⅓ brandy
⅓ curaçao
⅓ anisette
1 egg yolk
Shake well with ice and strain
into glass.

Normandy (for 4–6)
3 jiggers brandy
2 jiggers calvados or apple
brandy
1 jigger dry gin
4 jiggers sweet cider
Shake well with ice and strain
into glasses.

Odd McIntyre
¼ brandy
¼ Cointreau
¼ Lillet
¼ lemon juice
Stir well with ice and strain into
glass.

Old-Fashioned (Brandy)
Place lump of sugar in bottom of
old-fashioned glass. Sprinkle
with 1 dash of Angostura bitters.
Add twist of lemon peel and ice
cubes and fill as desired with
brandy. Stir and serve. (See
Index.)

Olympic
⅓ brandy
⅓ curaçao

⅓ orange juice
Stir well with ice and strain into
glass.

Palm Tree
1 oz. cognac
1 oz. Luxardo
3 oz. Byrrh
Stir with ice and strain into glass.

Peter Tower
⅔ brandy
⅓ light rum
1 teaspoon grenadine
1 teaspoon curaçao
1 teaspoon lemon juice
Shake well with ice and strain
into glass.

Phoebe Snow
½ brandy
½ Dubonnet
1 dash Pernod
Stir well with ice and strain into
glass.

Poop Deck
See LET'S SLIDE, above.

Pousse Café
[Note: This can be made of
different sets of ingredients, of
different specific gravities,
poured heaviest first, then the
next heaviest, etc., so as to produce a layered drink of different
colors.]
¼ jigger grenadine
¼ jigger maraschino
¼ jigger green crème de menthe
¼ jigger crème de violette
¼ jigger green Chartreuse
¼ jigger brandy

Pour ingredients one at a time, in order listed, into glass.

or

¼ jigger maraschino
¼ jigger raspberry syrup
¼ jigger crème de cacao
¼ jigger curaçao
¼ jigger yellow Chartreuse
¼ jigger brandy

Pour ingredients one at a time, in order listed, into glass.

Prairie Oyster

1 jigger brandy
1 egg
1 dash Worcestershire sauce
Salt if desired

Carefully break egg into 6-oz. glass. Add Worcestershire sauce and brandy. Blend lightly with egg white, keeping yolk intact. For the morning after. (See Index.)

Presto

⅔ brandy
⅓ sweet vermouth
1 dash orange juice
1 dash Pernod

Stir well with ice and strain into glass.

Quaker's

⅓ brandy
⅓ rum
⅙ lemon juice
⅙ raspberry syrup

Shake well with ice and strain into glass.

Queen Elizabeth (Brandy)

2 oz. cognac
2 oz. sweet vermouth

1 dash curaçao

Stir well with ice and strain into glass. Garnish with a cherry. (See Index.)

Quelle Vie

⅔ brandy
⅓ kümmel

Stir well with ice and strain into glass.

Saratoga No. 1

2 jiggers brandy
2 dashes maraschino
2 dashes Angostura bitters
¼ slice pineapple

Shake well with ice and strain. Add a little club soda if desired.

Saucy Sue

½ brandy
½ calvados or apple brandy
1 dash apricot brandy
1 dash Pernod

Stir well with ice and strain into glass. Squeeze orange peel over top.

Savoy Hotel

⅓ brandy
⅓ Bénédictine
⅓ crème de cacao

Pour ingredients carefully into liqueur glass so that they do not mix. Serve after dinner.

Sidecar (Brandy)

½ brandy
¼ Cointreau
¼ lemon juice

Shake well with ice and strain into glass. (See Index.)

Sink or Swim
¾ brandy
¼ sweet vermouth
1 dash Angostura bitters
Stir well with ice and strain into
glass.

Sir Ridgeway Knight
⅔ jigger brandy
⅔ jigger Triple Sec
⅔ jigger yellow Chartreuse
2 dashes Angostura bitters
Shake well with ice and strain
into glass.

Sir Walter
⅔ brandy
⅓ light rum
1 teaspoon grenadine
1 teaspoon curaçao
1 teaspoon lemon juice
Shake well with ice and strain
into glass.

Sledge Hammer
⅓ brandy
⅓ rum
⅓ apple brandy
1 dash Pernod
Shake well with ice and strain
into glass.

Sleepy Head
2 jiggers brandy
1 twist orange peel
4 leaves fresh mint, slightly
crushed
1–2 ice cubes
Combine in old-fashioned glass
and fill with ginger ale.

Southern Cross
1 jigger brandy

1 jigger medium rum
Juice of ½ lime
½ teaspoon sugar
1 dash curaçao
Shake well with ice and strain
into large cocktail glass. Add
dollop of club soda.

Southern Rebel
1 oz. cognac
1 oz. Irish Mist
1 oz. Southern Comfort
1 oz. lemon juice
Few drops grenadine
Mix in a cocktail glass with
cracked ice.

Stinger (Brandy)
½ brandy
½ white crème de menthe
Shake well with shaved ice and
strain into glass. (See Index.)

Stomach Reviver
⅓ brandy
⅓ kümmel
⅙ Angostura bitters
⅙ Fernet Branca
Stir well with ice and strain into
glass. (For the morning after.)

Sweeney's
1 jigger brandy
⅓ jigger pineapple juice
1 dash maraschino
3 dashes Angostura bitters
Shake well with ice and strain
into glass.

Tantalus
⅓ brandy
⅓ Forbidden Fruit
⅓ lemon juice

Shake well with ice and strain into glass.

Third Rail (Brandy)
⅓ brandy
⅓ calvados or apple brandy
⅓ light rum
1 dash Pernod
Shake well with ice and strain into glass. (See Index.)

Three
⅔ brandy
⅓ light rum
1 dash lemon juice
1 teaspoon grenadine
Stir well with ice and strain into glass.

Thunder and Lightning
2 jiggers brandy
1 teaspoon sugar syrup
1 egg yolk
1 pinch cayenne pepper
Shake well with ice and strain into a large cocktail glass.

Tin Wedding
¾ jigger brandy
¾ jigger dry gin
¾ jigger sweet vermouth
2 dashes orange bitters
Shake well with ice and strain into glass.

Vanderbilt Hotel
¾ brandy
¼ cherry brandy
2 dashes Angostura bitters
2 dashes sugar syrup
Stir well with ice and strain into glass.

Wallick's Special
1 jigger brandy
1 jigger cream
1 egg white
½ teaspoon powdered sugar
2 dashes grenadine
Shake well with ice and strain into glass.

Ward's
½ jigger brandy
½ jigger Chartreuse
Orange peel
Arrange the orange peel in bottom of glass to form a circle. Fill it with finely cracked ice and add the Chartreuse and brandy and decorate with fresh mint leaves. Different liqueurs may be used if desired.

Waterbury
2 jiggers brandy
1 egg white
Juice of ¼ lemon
½ teaspoon powdered sugar
2 dashes grenadine
Shake well with ice and strain into glass.

W.C.T.U.
1 jigger brandy
1 jigger dry vermouth
1 dash Angostura bitters
1 dash orange bitters
Shake quickly with shaved ice and strain into glass. Serve with a twist of lemon peel.

Whip
½ brandy
¼ sweet vermouth
¼ dry vermouth

3 dashes curaçao
1 dash Pernod
Shake well with ice and strain into glass.

White Way
⅓ brandy
⅓ anisette
⅓ Pernod
Stir well with ice and strain into glass.

Why Marry?
½ brandy
½ dry gin
1 dollop Cointreau
1 dollop lemon juice
Shake well with ice and strain into glass.

William of Orange
⅔ brandy
⅓ curaçao
1 dash orange bitters
Stir well with ice and strain into glass.

Willie Smith
⅔ brandy
⅓ maraschino
1 dash lemon juice
Stir well with ice and strain into glass.

W. Johnson Quinn
½ brandy
¼ sweet vermouth
¼ dry vermouth
3 dashes curaçao
1 dash grenadine
Stir well with ice and strain into glass.

Yes and No
2 jiggers brandy
4 dashes curaçao
1 egg white
Shake well with ice and strain into glass. Sprinkle with a grating of nutmeg.

Young Man
¾ brandy
¼ sweet vermouth
2 dashes curaçao
1 dash Angostura bitters
Stir well with ice and strain into glass.

Zinger (for 2)
2 oz. brandy
2 oz. CocoRibe
Stir. Serve over ice in a brandy snifter.

Zoom
1½ jiggers brandy
⅓ jigger honey
½ jigger cream
Shake with ice and strain into glass.

COCKTAILS—CALVADOS AND KIRSCH BASES

CALVADOS

[Note: Calvados, applejack, and apple brandy may be used interchangeably.]

A.J.
½ calvados
½ unsweetened grapefruit juice
Grenadine to taste
Shake well with ice and strain into glass.

Ante
½ calvados
¼ Cointreau
¼ Dubonnet
1 dash Angostura bitters
Stir well with ice and strain into glass.

Apple
⅓ calvados
⅙ brandy
⅙ gin
⅓ sweet cider
Stir well with ice and strain into glass.

Applejack No. 1
1 jigger applejack
1 teaspoon sugar syrup
2 dashes orange bitters
1 dash Angostura bitters
Stir well with ice and strain into glass.

Applejack No. 2
¾ applejack
¼ sweet vermouth
1 dash Angostura bitters
Stir well with ice and strain into glass.

Applejack Rabbit
1 jigger applejack
⅓ jigger lemon juice
⅓ jigger orange juice
Maple syrup to taste
Shake well with ice and strain into glass.

Applejack Sour
2 jiggers applejack
Juice of ½ lime
Juice of ½ lemon
1 dash grenadine
½ teaspoon sugar
Shake well with ice and strain into Delmonico glass. Decorate with fruit if desired.

Barton Special
½ calvados
¼ Scotch whisky
¼ dry gin
Shake well with ice and strain into glass. Serve with twist of lemon peel.

Bentley
½ calvados
½ Dubonnet
Stir well with ice and strain into glass.

Calvados
⅓ calvados
⅓ orange juice
⅙ Cointreau
⅙ orange bitters
Stir well with ice and strain into glass.

Castle Dip
½ apple brandy
½ white crème de menthe
3 dashes Pernod
Shake well with ice and strain into glass.

Depth Bomb
1 jigger applejack
1 jigger brandy
¼ teaspoon grenadine
¼ teaspoon lemon juice
Shake well with ice and strain into glass.

Dick Molnar (Diki-Diki)
⅔ calvados
⅙ Swedish punsch
⅙ grapefruit juice
Stir well with ice and strain into glass.

Honeymoon
1 jigger applejack
½ jigger Bénédictine
Juice of ½ lemon
3 dashes curaçao
Shake well with ice and strain into glass.

Jack-in-the-Box
1 jigger applejack
½ jigger pineapple juice
Juice of ½ lemon
2 dashes Angostura bitters
Shake well with ice and strain into glass.

Jack Rose
1 jigger applejack
⅓ jigger grenadine
Juice of ½ lime
Shake well with ice and strain into glass.

Jersey Lightning
2 jiggers applejack
1 dash Angostura bitters
Sugar syrup to taste
Shake well with ice and strain into glass.

Kenny (for 4)
3 jiggers applejack
2 jiggers sweet vermouth
Juice of ½ lemon
1 dash Angostura bitters
2 dashes grenadine
Shake well with ice and strain into glasses.

Liberty
⅔ applejack
⅓ light rum
1 dash sugar syrup
Shake well with ice and strain into glass.

Oom Paul
½ calvados
½ Dubonnet
1 dash Angostura bitters
Stir well with ice and strain into glass.

Philadelphia Scotchman
⅓ applejack
⅓ port
⅓ orange juice
Place in large cocktail glass with cracked ice and fill with club soda.

Princess Mary's Pride
½ calvados
¼ Dubonnet
¼ dry vermouth
Stir well with ice and strain into glass.

Roulette
½ calvados
¼ light rum
¼ Swedish punsch

Stir well with ice and strain into glass.

Royal Smile
½ applejack
¼ dry gin
¼ grenadine
Juice of ¼ lemon
Shake well with ice and strain into glass.

Sharkey Punch
¾ calvados
¼ rye whiskey
1 teaspoon sugar syrup
Shake well with ice and strain into glass. Add dash of club soda.

Special Rough
½ applejack
½ brandy
1 dash Pernod
Stir with shaved ice and strain into glass.

Star No. 1
½ applejack
½ sweet vermouth
1 dash orange bitters
Stir with cracked ice and strain into glass. Sugar syrup may be added if desired.

Stone Fence (Applejack)
2 jiggers applejack
1–2 dashes Angostura bitters
Place in tall glass with ice and fill with cider. (See Index.)

Tinton
⅔ applejack
⅓ port wine

Stir well with ice and strain into glass.

Torpedo
⅔ calvados
⅓ brandy
1 dash gin
Stir well with ice and strain into glass.

Tulip
⅓ calvados
⅓ sweet vermouth
⅙ apricot brandy
⅙ lemon juice
Stir well with ice and strain into glass.

Twelve Miles Out
⅓ calvados
⅓ light rum
⅓ Swedish punsch
Stir well with ice and strain into glass. Squeeze orange peel over top.

Whist
½ calvados
¼ light rum
¼ sweet vermouth
Stir well with ice and strain into glass.

Widow's Kiss
½ calvados
¼ yellow Chartreuse
¼ Bénédictine
1 dash Angostura bitters
Shake well with ice and strain into glass.

KIRSCH

Café Kirsch
1 jigger kirsch
1 teaspoon sugar
2 jiggers cold coffee
1 egg white
Shake well with ice and strain into glass.

Rose No. 3
½ kirsch
½ dry vermouth
1 teaspoon grenadine
Stir well with ice and strain into glass. (See Index.)

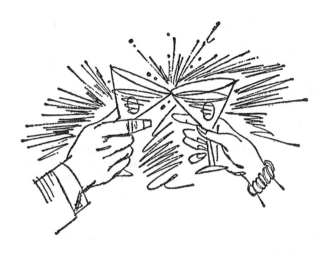

COCKTAILS—GIN BASE

Abbey
½ dry gin
¼ Lillet
¼ orange juice
1 dash Angostura bitters
Stir well with ice and strain into glass. Serve with a twist of orange peel or a cherry.

Absinthe
1 jigger gin
⅔ jigger Pernod
1 dash Angostura
1 dash grenadine
Shake with cracked ice.

Alaska
¾ dry gin
¼ yellow Chartreuse
2 dashes orange bitters
Stir well with ice and strain into glass. Serve with a twist of lemon peel.

Alexander (Gin)
½ dry gin
¼ crème de cacao
¼ cream
Shake well with ice and strain into glass. (See Index.)

Alexander's Sister
½ dry gin
¼ crème de menthe
¼ cream
Shake well with ice and strain into glass.

Alfonso Special (Gin)
¼ dry gin
¼ dry vermouth
½ Grand Marnier
4 dashes sweet vermouth
1 dash Angostura bitters
Shake well with ice and strain into glass. (See Index.)

Allen Special
⅔ dry gin
⅓ maraschino
1 dash lemon juice
Stir well with ice and strain into glass.

Allies
½ dry gin
½ dry vermouth
2 dashes kümmel
Stir well with ice and strain into glass.

Angel Face
⅓ dry gin
⅓ apricot brandy
⅓ calvados or apple brandy
Stir well with ice and strain into glass.

Apparent
½ dry gin
½ Dubonnet
1 dash Pernod
Shake well with ice and strain into glass.

Astoria (Hoffman House)
⅔ dry gin
⅓ dry vermouth
1 dash orange bitters
Stir well with ice and strain into glass. Serve with an olive.

Attention
¼ dry gin
¼ Pernod
¼ dry vermouth
¼ crème de violette
2 dashes orange bitters
Stir well with ice and strain into glass.

Aviation
⅔ dry gin
⅓ lemon juice
2 dashes maraschino
2 dashes apricot brandy
Stir well with ice and strain into glass.

Barbary Coast
¼ dry gin
¼ Scotch whisky
¼ crème de cacao
¼ cream
Shake well with ice and strain into small highball or old-fashioned glass.

Barnum
⅔ dry gin
⅓ apricot brandy
2 dashes Angostura bitters
1 dash lemon or lime juice
Shake well with ice and strain into glass.

Baron
⅔ dry gin
⅓ dry vermouth
6 dashes curaçao
2 dashes sweet vermouth
Stir well with ice and strain into glass. Serve with a twist of lemon peel.

Beauty Spot
⅔ gin
⅓ grenadine
1 egg white
Shake well with ice and strain into glass.

Bees' Knees

1 jigger gin
1 teaspoon honey
Juice of ¼ lemon
Shake well with ice and strain into glass.

Belmont

⅔ gin
⅓ grenadine or raspberry syrup
½ jigger cream
Shake well with ice and strain into glass.

Bennett

¾ dry gin
¼ lime juice
1–2 dashes Angostura bitters
1 teaspoon powdered sugar (optional)
Shake well with ice and strain into glass.

Bermuda Rose

1 jigger dry gin
1 dash grenadine
1 dash apricot brandy
⅓ jigger lemon or lime juice
Shake well with ice and strain into glass.

Berry Wall

½ dry gin
½ sweet vermouth
4 dashes curaçao
Stir with ice and strain into glass. Twist a lemon peel just over the top and serve with a cherry.

Bich's Special

⅔ dry gin
⅓ Lillet
1 dash Angostura bitters
Stir well with ice and strain into glass. Squeeze orange peel over top.

Biffy

½ dry gin
¼ Swedish punsch
¼ lemon juice
Stir well with ice and strain into glass.

Bijou

⅓ dry gin
⅓ green Chartreuse
⅓ sweet vermouth
1 dash orange bitters
Stir well with ice and strain into glass. Serve with a twist of lemon peel.

Bill Lyken's Delight

½ dry gin
½ sweet vermouth
4 dashes curaçao
1 twist lemon peel
1 twist orange peel
Stir well with ice and strain into glass.

Bitter

½ dry gin
¼ lemon juice
¼ green Chartreuse
1 dash Pernod
Shake well with ice and strain into glass. A pinch of sugar may be added if desired.

Blackthorn (Gin)

½ sloe gin
½ sweet vermouth
2 dashes orange bitters
Stir well with ice and strain into

glass. Twist lemon peel over top and serve with a cherry. (See Index.)

Bloodhound
½ dry gin
¼ dry vermouth
¼ sweet vermouth
2–3 crushed strawberries
Stir well with ice and strain into glass.

Bloody Mary (Gin)
1 jigger gin
2 jiggers tomato juice
⅓ jigger lemon juice
1 dash Worcestershire sauce
Salt and pepper
1 dash Tabasco
Shake well and strain into large glass. (See Index.)

Blue Bird
2 jiggers dry gin
4 dashes Angostura bitters
4 dashes curaçao
Stir well with ice and strain into glass. Twist lemon peel over top and serve with a cherry.

Blue Devil
½ dry gin
¼ maraschino
¼ lemon or lime juice
1 dash blue curaçao
Shake well with ice and strain into glass.

Blue Moon
1 jigger dry gin
⅓ jigger maraschino
1 egg white
Shake well with ice and strain into glass.

Blue Train (Gin)
½ dry gin
¼ lemon juice
¼ Cointreau
1 dash blue curaçao
Shake well with ice and strain into glass. (See Index.)

Bon Appetit
½ dry gin
½ Dubonnet
3 dashes Angostura bitters
Juice of ½ orange
Shake well with ice and strain into glass.

Breakfast
⅔ dry gin
⅓ grenadine
1 egg white
Shake well with ice and strain into glass.

Bronx (dry)
¾ dry gin
¼ dry vermouth
Juice of ¼ orange
Stir well with ice and strain into glass.

Bronx (sweet)
½ dry gin
¼ dry vermouth
¼ sweet vermouth
Juice of ¼ orange
Stir well with ice and strain into glass.

Bronx Golden
Prepare same as BRONX (SWEET), adding yolk of 1 egg.

Bronx River
⅔ jigger dry gin
⅓ jigger sweet vermouth
Juice of 1 lemon
½ teaspoon sugar
Stir well with ice and strain into glass.

Bronx Silver (Oriental)
Prepare same as BRONX (SWEET), adding the white of 1 egg and 1 slice pineapple.

Buby
½ dry gin
½ lemon juice
1 teaspoon grenadine
Shake well and strain into glass.

Bulldog (Gin)
Place 2–3 cubes in a large old-fashioned glass. Add 2 jiggers gin, the juice of 1 orange and fill with ginger ale. Stir slightly and serve, sometimes with a straw. (See Index.)

Bunny Hug
⅓ dry gin
⅓ whiskey (Bourbon or blend)
⅓ Pernod
Shake well with ice and strain into glass.

B.V.D.
⅓ dry gin
⅓ light rum
⅓ dry vermouth
Stir well with ice and strain into glass.

Cabaret
½ dry gin
½ Dubonnet
1 dash Pernod
1 dash Angostura bitters
Stir well with ice and strain into glass. Serve with a cherry.

Café de Paris
2 jiggers dry gin
3 dashes anisette
1 teaspoon cream
1 egg white
Shake well with ice and strain into glass.

Campden
½ dry gin
¼ Cointreau
¼ Lillet
Stir well with ice and strain into glass. Serve with a cherry.

Caruso
⅓ dry gin
⅓ dry vermouth
⅓ green crème de menthe
Stir well with ice and strain into glass.

Casino
2 jiggers Old Tom gin
2 dashes maraschino
2 dashes orange bitters
2 dashes lemon juice
Stir well with ice and strain into glass.

Cat's Eye
⅓ jigger dry gin
⅙ jigger lemonade
⅙ teaspoon kirsch
⅓ jigger dry vermouth
1 dash Cointreau

Shake well with ice and strain into glass. Serve with a twist of lemon peel.

C.F.H.
⅓ dry gin
⅙ calvados or apple brandy
⅙ Swedish punsch
⅙ grenadine
⅙ lemon juice
Shake well with ice and strain into glass.

Chanticleer
2 jiggers dry gin
Juice of ½ lemon
1 tablespoon raspberry syrup
1 egg white
Shake well with ice and strain into glass.

Chappelle
Muddle 2–3 slices of pineapple in a shaker. Add ½ jigger sweet vermouth, ½ jigger dry gin, and the juice of ½ lime. Shake well with ice and strain into glass.

Charleston
⅙ dry gin
⅙ kirsch
⅙ maraschino
⅙ curaçao
⅙ dry vermouth
⅙ sweet vermouth
Stir well with ice and strain into glass. Squeeze lemon peel over top.

Charlie Lindbergh
½ dry gin
½ Lillet
2 dashes apricot brandy

2 dashes orange juice
Stir well with ice and strain into glass. Squeeze lemon peel over top.

Chatterley
½ dry gin
¼ dry vermouth
⅛ orange juice
⅛ curaçao
Shake well with ice and strain into glass.

Claridge
⅓ dry gin
⅓ dry vermouth
⅙ apricot brandy
⅙ Cointreau
Stir well with ice and strain into glass. Serve with a cherry.

Clover Club
⅔ dry gin
⅓ grenadine
Juice of ½ lime
1 egg white
Shake well with ice and strain into glass.

Club
⅔ dry gin
⅓ sweet vermouth
Stir well with ice and strain into glass. Serve with a cherry or an olive.

Cordova
⅔ dry gin
⅓ sweet vermouth
1 dash Pernod
1 teaspoon cream
Shake well with ice and strain into glass.

Cornell
1 jigger dry gin
3 dashes maraschino
1 egg white
Shake well with ice and strain
into glass.

Corpse Reviver No. 2
¼ dry gin
¼ Cointreau
¼ Swedish punsch
¼ lemon juice
1 dash Pernod
Shake well with ice and strain
into glass. (See Index.)

Darb
⅓ dry gin
⅓ dry vermouth
⅓ apricot brandy
4 dashes lemon juice
Stir well with ice and strain into
glass.

Darby
1 jigger dry gin
⅓ jigger lime juice
⅓ jigger grapefruit juice
1 teaspoon powdered sugar
Shake well with ice and strain
into a large cocktail glass. Top
with a squirt of club soda and
add a cherry.

Deep Sea
½ Old Tom gin
½ dry vermouth
1 dash Pernod
1 dash orange bitters
Stir well with ice and strain into
glass. Squeeze lemon peel over
top and serve with an olive.

Dempsey
½ dry gin
½ calvados or apple brandy
2 dashes Pernod
2 dashes grenadine
Stir well with ice and strain into
glass.

Depth Charge
½ dry gin
½ Lillet
2 dashes Pernod
Shake well with ice and strain
into glass. Squeeze orange peel
over top.

Desert Healer
2 jiggers dry gin
⅓ jigger cherry brandy
Juice of 1 orange
Shake well with ice and strain
into tall glass. Fill with cold ginger beer.

Devonia
⅓ jigger dry gin
⅔ jigger sparkling cider
2 dashes orange bitters
Stir lightly with cracked ice and
strain into glass.

Diabola
⅓ dry gin
⅔ Dubonnet
2 dashes orgeat syrup
Stir well with ice and strain into
glass. Serve with a cherry.

Dixie
½ jigger dry gin
¼ jigger Pernod
¼ jigger dry vermouth
Juice of ¼ orange

2 dashes grenadine
Shake well with ice and strain
into glass.

Dodge Special
½ dry gin
½ Cointreau
1 dash grape juice
Stir well with ice and strain into
glass.

Dolly O'Dare
½ dry gin
½ dry vermouth
6 dashes apricot brandy
Stir well with ice and strain into
glass. Squeeze orange peel over
top.

D.O.M.
¾ dry gin
⅛ orange juice
⅛ Bénédictine
Shake well with ice and strain
into glass.

Du Barry
⅔ dry gin
⅓ dry vermouth
2 dashes Pernod
1 dash Angostura bitters
Stir well with ice and strain into
glass. Serve with thin slice of orange.

Dunhill's Special
⅓ jigger dry gin
⅓ jigger sherry
⅓ jigger dry vermouth
1 tablespoon curaçao
Stir well with ice and strain into
glasses with 2 dashes Pernod and
an olive in each.

Eagle's Dream
¾ dry gin
¼ Crème Yvette
Juice of ¼ lemon
1 egg white
1 teaspoon powdered sugar
Shake well with ice and strain
into glass.

Earthquake
⅓ dry gin
⅓ whiskey
⅓ Pernod
Shake well with ice and strain
into glass. (It's been said by
those who know that one of
these should be sufficient.)

Eclipse
⅓ dry gin
⅔ sloe gin
Place a cherry or ripe olive in a
cocktail glass and add enough
grenadine to cover. Shake the
gins with ice and strain slowly
into the glass so that they *do not*
mix with the grenadine. Squeeze
an orange peel over the top.

Eddie Brown
⅔ dry gin
⅓ Lillet
2 dashes apricot brandy
Stir well with ice and strain into
glass. Squeeze lemon peel over
top.

Elegant
½ dry gin
½ dry vermouth
2 dashes Grand Marnier
Stir well with ice and serve.

Emerald

⅓ jigger dry gin
⅓ jigger green Chartreuse
⅓ jigger sweet vermouth
1 teaspoon orange bitters
Shake well with ice and strain
into glass. Serve with a cherry
and a twist of lemon peel.

Empire

½ dry gin
¼ calvados or apple brandy
¼ apricot brandy
Stir well with ice and strain into
glass. Serve with a cherry.

E. Nos

⅔ dry gin
⅓ dry vermouth
3 dashes Pernod
Stir well with ice and strain into
glass. Serve with a cherry.

Eton Blazer

¾ dry gin
¼ kirsch
½ tablespoon powdered sugar
Juice of ½ lemon
Shake well with ice and strain
into large cocktail glass. Fill with
club soda.

Fairbanks

⅓ dry gin
⅓ dry vermouth
⅓ apricot brandy
1 dash lemon juice
1 dash grenadine
Stir well with ice and strain into
glass. Serve with a cherry.

Fairy Belle

¾ dry gin
¼ apricot brandy
1 teaspoon grenadine
1 egg white
Shake well with ice and strain
into glass.

Fallen Angel

2 jiggers dry gin
Juice of 1 lemon or lime
2 dashes crème de menthe
1 dash Angostura bitters
Stir well with ice and strain into
glass. Serve with a cherry.

Fall River

⅓ dry gin
⅓ brandy
⅙ white crème de menthe
⅙ maraschino
Shake well with ice and strain
into glass.

Fascinator

⅔ dry gin
⅓ dry vermouth
2 dashes Pernod
1 sprig fresh mint
Shake well with ice and strain
into glass.

Favourite

⅓ dry gin
⅓ dry vermouth
⅓ apricot brandy
1 dash lemon juice
Stir well with ice and strain into
glass. Serve with a cherry.

Fifth Avenue
½ dry gin
¼ sweet vermouth
¼ Fernet Branca
Stir well with ice and strain into glass.

Fifty-Fifty
½ dry gin
½ dry vermouth
Stir well with cracked ice and strain into glass. Serve with an olive.

Fine and Dandy
½ dry gin
¼ Cointreau
¼ lemon juice
1 dash Angostura bitters
Stir well with ice and strain into glass. Serve with a cherry.

Frankenjack
⅓ dry gin
⅓ dry vermouth
⅙ apricot brandy
⅙ Cointreau
Stir well with ice and strain into glass. Serve with a cherry.

French Rose
⅔ jigger dry gin
⅓ jigger cherry brandy
⅓ jigger cherry liqueur
Shake well with ice and strain into glass.

Gene Tunney
⅔ dry gin
⅓ dry vermouth
1 dash orange juice
1 dash lemon juice
Stir well with ice and strain into glass. Serve with a cherry.

Gibson
4 parts dry gin (or more)
1 part dry vermouth (or less)
Stir well with ice and strain into glass. Serve with a pickled pearl onion.

Gilroy
⅓ dry gin
⅓ cherry brandy
⅙ dry vermouth
⅙ lemon juice
1 dash orange bitters
Stir well with ice and strain into glass.

Gimlet
¾ dry gin
¼ lime juice
Stir well with ice and strain into large glass. Fill with club soda.

Gimlet (Gin)
½ dry gin
½ Rose's lime juice
Stir with ice and strain into glass. (See Index.)

Gin and Bitters (Pink Gin)
2 jiggers dry gin
1 dash Angostura bitters
Pour over ice in glass and serve.

Gin and Sin
¾ gin
⅛ orange juice
⅛ lemon juice
1 dash grenadine
Shake well with ice and strain into glass.

Gin and Tonic
2 jiggers gin
Juice ½ lemon
Pour over ice in a tall glass. Fill
up with tonic water.

Gin Ho (Gin-on-the-Rocks)
Fill an old-fashioned glass with
cracked ice. Pour on the amount
of gin desired and serve. A twist
of lemon peel may be added.

Gin Rickey
See RICKEYS

Gin Sour
¾ dry gin
¼ lemon juice
1 teaspoon sugar
Shake well with ice. Strain into a
sour glass.

Golden Clipper
¼ dry gin
¼ light rum
¼ preach brandy
¼ orange juice
Shake well with ice and strain
into glass.

Golden Dawn
⅔ jigger dry gin
½ jigger orange juice
⅓ jigger apricot brandy
Shake well with ice and strain
into glass.

Golf
⅔ dry gin
⅓ dry vermouth
2 dashes Angostura bitters
Stir well with ice and strain into
glass. Serve with an olive.

Grand Royal Clover Club
2 jiggers dry gin
1 tablespoon grenadine
Juice of ½ lemon
1 egg
Shake well with ice and strain
into glass.

Grapefruit
3 parts dry gin
1 part grapefruit juice
Shake well with ice and strain
into glass.

Grape Vine
½ dry gin
¼ grape juice
¼ lemon juice
1 dash grenadine
Stir well with ice and strain into
glass.

Great Secret
⅔ dry gin
⅓ Lillet
1 dash Angostura bitters
Stir well with ice and strain into
glass. Serve with twist of orange
peel.

Green Dragon No. 1
½ dry gin
⅛ kümmel
¼ crème de menthe
⅛ lemon juice
4 dashes peach bitters
Shake well with ice and strain
into glass. (See Index.)

Guards
⅔ dry gin
⅓ sweet vermouth
2 dashes curaçao

Stir well with ice and strain into glass. Serve with twist of orange peel or a cherry.

Gunga Din
¾ dry gin
¼ dry vermouth
1 wedge pineapple
Juice of ¼ orange
Shake well with ice and strain into glass.

Hakam
½ dry gin
½ sweet vermouth
2 dashes curaçao
1 dash orange bitters
Stir well with ice and strain into glass. Serve with a cherry.

Hanky-Panky
⅔ dry gin
⅓ sweet vermouth
2 dashes Fernet Branca
Stir well with ice and strain into glass. Serve with twist of orange peel.

Harry's
⅔ dry gin
⅓ sweet vermouth
1 dash Pernod
2 dashes crème de menthe
Shake well with ice and strain into glass. Serve with a mint leaf or two if in season.

Have a Heart
1 jigger dry gin
½ jigger Swedish punsch
2 dashes grenadine
Juice of ½ lime
Shake well with shaved ice and

strain into glass. Serve with a wedge of pineapple and a cherry.

Hawaiian No. 1
1 jigger dry gin
½ jigger pineapple juice
1 dash orange bitters
1 egg white
Shake well with ice and strain into glass.

Hawaiian No. 2
4 parts dry gin
1 part orange juice
1 part curaçao
Shake well with ice and strain into glass.

Hoffman House
See ASTORIA.

Holland House
⅔ dry gin
⅓ dry vermouth
Juice of ¼ lemon
1 wedge pineapple
4 dashes maraschino
Stir well with ice and strain into glass.

Honolulu
⅓ dry gin
⅓ Bénédictine
⅓ maraschino
Stir well with ice and strain into glass.

H.P.W.
½ Old Tom gin
½ dry vermouth
Stir well with ice and strain into glass. Serve with twist of orange peel.

Hula-Hula
⅔ dry gin
⅓ orange juice
1 dash curaçao
Shake well with ice and strain
into glass.

Hurricane
⅓ dry gin
⅓ whiskey
⅓ crème de menthe
Juice of ½ lemon
Shake well with ice and strain
into glass.

Ideal
⅔ dry gin
⅓ sweet vermouth
3 dashes maraschino
1 tablespoon grapefruit juice
Shake well with ice and strain
into glass.

Inca
¼ dry gin
¼ dry sherry
¼ dry vermouth
¼ sweet vermouth
1 dash orgeat syrup
1 dash orange bitters
Stir well with ice and strain into
glass.

Jabberwock
⅓ dry gin
⅓ dry sherry
⅓ Dubonnet
2 dashes orange bitters
Stir well with ice and drain into
glass. Squeeze lemon peel over
top and serve with a cherry.

Jack Kearns
¾ dry gin
¼ light rum
4 dashes sugar syrup
1 dash lemon juice
Shake well with ice and strain
into glass. (This may be made
with less sugar syrup if desired.)

Jack Pine
¾ dry gin
¼ dry vermouth
1 slice pineapple
Juice of ¼ orange
Shake well with ice and strain
into glass.

Jackson
½ dry gin
½ Dubonnet
2 dashes orange bitters
Stir well with ice and strain into
glass.

Jewel
⅓ dry gin
⅓ green Chartreuse
⅓ sweet vermouth
1 dash orange bitters
Shake well with ice and strain
into glass. Serve with twist of
lemon peel and, if you want, a
cherry.

Jeyplak
⅔ dry gin
⅓ sweet vermouth
1 dash Pernod
Stir well with ice and strain into
glass. Twist lemon peel over top
and serve with a cherry.

Jockey Club
1½ jiggers dry gin
1 dash orange bitters
1 dash Angostura bitters
2 dashes crème de noyau
4 dashes lemon juice
Stir well with ice and strain into glass.

Johnnie Mack
⅔ sloe gin
⅓ curaçao
3 dashes Pernod
Stir well with ice and strain into glass. Serve with twist of lemon peel.

J.O.S.
⅓ dry gin
⅓ dry vermouth
⅓ sweet vermouth
1 dash brandy
1 dash orange bitters
1 dash lemon or lime juice
Stir well with ice and strain into glass. Twist lemon peel over top.

Judge Jr.
⅓ dry gin
⅓ light rum
⅓ lemon juice
1–3 dashes grenadine
Shake well with ice and strain into glass. Powdered sugar may be added if more sweetness is desired.

Judgette
⅓ dry gin
⅓ peach brandy
⅓ dry vermouth
1 dash lime juice

Stir well with ice and strain.
Serve with a cherry if desired.

K.C.B.
¾ dry gin
¼ kirsch
1 dash apricot brandy
1 dash lemon juice
Stir well with ice and strain into glass. Serve with twist of lemon peel.

Lady Finger
½ dry gin
¼ kirsch
¼ cherry brandy
Stir well with ice and strain into glass.

Lasky
⅓ dry gin
⅓ Swedish punsch
⅓ grape juice
Shake well with ice and strain into glass.

Leap Frog (London Buck)
1 jigger dry gin
Juice of ½ lemon
Cracked ice
Place all together in a large cocktail glass and fill with ginger ale or ginger beer.

Leap Year
⅔ dry gin
⅙ sweet vermouth
⅙ Grand Marnier
1 dash lemon juice
Stir well with ice and strain into glass. Squeeze lemon peel over top.

Leave It to Me

½ dry gin
¼ dry vermouth
¼ apricot brandy
1 dash lemon juice
1 dash grenadine
Stir well with ice and strain into glass.

Leo Special

½ dry gin
¼ lime juice
¼ Cointreau
2 dashes Pernod
Stir well with ice and strain into glass.

Lilly

⅓ dry gin
⅓ crème de noyau
⅓ Lillet
1 dash lemon juice
Stir with ice and strain into glass.

Little Devil

⅓ dry gin
⅓ light rum
⅙ Cointreau
⅙ lemon juice
Stir well with ice and strain into glass.

London

1 jigger dry gin
2 dashes maraschino
2 dashes sugar syrup
2 dashes orange bitters
Stir well with ice and strain into glass. Serve with twist of lemon peel.

London Buck

See LEAP FROG.

Lord Suffolk

⅝ dry gin
⅛ Cointreau
⅛ sweet vermouth
⅛ maraschino
Stir well with ice and strain into glass. Serve with twist of lemon peel.

Loud Speaker

⅜ dry gin
⅜ brandy
⅛ Cointreau
⅛ lemon juice
Stir well with ice and strain into glass.

Luigi

½ dry gin
½ dry vermouth
Juice of ½ tangerine
1 dash Cointreau
1 teaspoon grenadine
Stir with ice and strain into glass. Serve with lemon peel.

Mabel Berra

½ jigger sloe gin
½ jigger Swedish punsch
Juice of ½ lime
Shake well with ice and strain into glass.

Mah-Jongg

⅔ dry gin
⅙ light rum
⅙ Cointreau
Stir well with ice and strain into glass. Serve with lemon twist.

Maiden's Blush (Maiden's Delight)
2 jiggers dry gin
4 dashes curaçao
4 dashes grenadine
1–2 dashes lemon juice
Shake well with ice and strain into glass.

Maiden's Prayer
⅜ dry gin
⅜ Cointreau
⅛ lemon juice
⅛ orange juice
Stir well with ice and strain into glass.

Manyann
½ dry gin
½ Dubonnet
2 dashes curaçao
Juice of 1 lemon
Shake well with ice and strain into glass.

Marny
⅔ dry gin
⅓ Grand Marnier
Stir well with ice and strain into glass. Serve with a cherry.

Martinez (for 6)
6 jiggers dry gin
4 jiggers dry vermouth
4 teaspoons curaçao or maraschino
1 teaspoon orange bitters
Shake with ice and strain into glasses. Serve with a twist of lemon peel and, if desired, a cherry in each.

Martini (dry)
5 or 6 parts dry gin
1 part dry vermouth
Stir with ice and strain into chilled glass. Serve with an olive. (See Index.)

Martini (medium)
2 to 4 parts dry gin
1 part dry vermouth
Stir with ice and strain into chilled glass. Serve with twist of lemon peel or an olive.

Martini (sweet)
6 parts dry gin
1 part dry vermouth
1 part sweet vermouth
Stir with ice and strain into chilled glass. Serve with an olive. A dash of orange bitters may be added.

Martini-on-the-Rocks
Pack an old-fashioned glass loosely with ice. Fill with dry gin and add a few dashes dry vermouth. Stir and serve. A twist of lemon peel may be added.

Mayfair
½ dry gin
¼ apricot brandy
¼ orange juice
Shake well with ice and strain into glass.

McClelland
⅔ sloe gin
⅓ curaçao
1 dash orange bitters
Stir well with ice and strain into glass.

Melon

2 oz. dry gin
1 oz. Midori
1 oz. lemon juice
Stir well with ice and strain into
glass. Serve with a cherry.

Merry Widow

½ dry gin
½ dry vermouth
2 dashes Bénédictine
1 dash Peychaud's bitters
2 dashes Pernod
Stir well with ice and strain into
glass. Serve with twist of lemon
peel.

Million Dollar

⅔ dry gin
⅓ sweet vermouth
1 tablespoon pineapple juice
1 teaspoon grenadine
1 egg white
Shake well with ice and strain
into glass.

Mint

⅜ dry gin
⅛ crème de menthe
½ white wine
Several sprigs of mint
Soak the mint for 2 hours in half
the wine. Add the other ingredients and remaining wine. Shake
well with ice and strain into
glass. Serve with sprig fresh mint
if in season.

Mississippi Mule

⅔ dry gin
⅙ lemon juice
⅙ crème de cassis

Stir well with ice and strain into
glass.

Mr. Eric Sutton's Gin Blind

6 parts dry gin
3 parts curaçao
2 parts brandy
1 dash orange bitters
Stir with ice and strain into glass.

Mr. Manhattan

2 jiggers dry gin
4 dashes orange juice
1 dash lemon juice
4 crushed mint leaves
1 lump sugar moistened with
water
Shake well with ice and strain
into glass.

Modern No. 1

⅔ sloe gin
⅓ Scotch whisky
1 dash Pernod
1 dash orange bitters
1 dash grenadine
Shake well with ice and strain
into glass. (See Index.)

Monkey Gland

⅔ dry gin
⅓ orange juice
3 dashes Bénédictine
3 dashes grenadine
Stir well with ice and strain into
glass.

Monte Carlo Imperial

½ dry gin
¼ lemon juice
¼ white crème de menthe
Shake well with ice and strain
into a large cocktail glass. Fill
with champagne.

Moonlight
⅓ dry gin
⅙ kirsch
⅙ grapefruit juice
⅓ white wine
Shake well with ice and strain
into glass. Serve with twist of
lemon peel.

Moulin Rouge
½ dry gin
⅜ apricot brandy
⅛ orange juice
3 dashes grenadine
Stir well with ice and strain into
glass.

Mule Hind Leg
⅕ dry gin
⅕ applejack
⅕ Bénédictine
⅕ maple syrup
⅕ apricot brandy
Stir well with ice and strain into
glass.

Napoleon
2 jiggers dry gin
1 dash Dubonnet
1 dash curaçao
1 dash Fernet Branca
Stir well with ice and strain into
glass. Squeeze lemon peel over
top.

Newbury
½ dry gin
½ sweet vermouth
3 dashes curaçao
1 twist lemon peel
1 twist orange peel
Stir well with ice and strain into
glass.

Nightmare
⅓ dry gin
⅓ Dubonnet
⅙ cherry brandy
⅙ orange juice
Shake well with ice and strain
into glass.

Noon
Prepare same as BRONX, adding
white of 1 egg.

Old Etonian
½ dry gin
½ Lillet
2 dashes orange bitters
2 dashes crème de noyau
Stir well with ice and strain into
glass. Serve with twist of orange
peel.

Old-Fashioned (Gin)
1–2 jiggers dry gin
1 slice lemon peel
½ piece lump sugar
1 dash Angostura bitters
Place sugar in bottom of old-
fashioned glass and sprinkle with
bitters. Crush. Add lemon and
ice cubes and fill with gin as desired. Stir and serve. (See
Index.)

Opal
½ dry gin
⅓ orange juice
⅙ Cointreau
¼ teaspoon powdered sugar
Shake well with ice and strain
into glass. A little orange flower
water may be added, if available.

Opera
⅔ dry gin
⅙ Dubonnet
⅙ maraschino
Stir well with ice and strain into glass. Squeeze orange peel over top.

Orange Bloom
½ dry gin
¼ sweet vermouth
¼ Cointreau
Stir with ice and strain into glass. Serve with a cherry.

Orange Blossom
2–3 jiggers dry gin
1 jigger orange juice
Stir well with cracked ice and strain into large cocktail glass. Powdered sugar or sugar syrup may be added if desired.

Orange Martini
½ dry gin
¼ dry vermouth
¼ sweet vermouth
1 orange rind, grated carefully
Steep the orange rind for 2 hours in the combined liquors. Shake well with ice and strain into glasses in each of which has been put a dash of orange bitters.

Oriental
See BRONX SILVER.

Pall Mall
⅓ dry gin
⅓ dry vermouth
⅓ sweet vermouth
1 teaspoon white crème de menthe

1 dash orange bitters
Stir well with ice and strain into glass.

Parisian
⅓ dry gin
⅓ dry vermouth
⅓ crème de cassis
Stir well with ice and strain into glass.

Pat's Special
⅓ dry gin
⅓ dry sherry
⅓ quinquina
2 dashes crème de cassis
2 dashes apricot brandy
Shake well with ice and strain into glass. Serve with a cherry and a piece of orange peel.

Pegu Club
⅔ dry gin
⅓ curaçao
1 dash orange bitters
1 dash Angostura bitters
1 teaspoon lime juice
Shake well with ice and strain into glass.

Perfect
⅓ dry gin
⅓ dry vermouth
⅓ sweet vermouth
Stir well with ice and strain into glass.

Piccadilly
⅔ dry gin
⅓ dry vermouth
1 dash Pernod
1 dash grenadine
Stir well with ice and strain into glass.

Ping-Pong Special

½ sloe gin
½ sweet vermouth
1 teaspoon Angostura bitters
2 teaspoons curaçao
Stir well with ice and strain into glass. Serve with a cherry and a twist of lemon peel.

Pink Gin

See GIN AND BITTERS.

Pink Lady

1 jigger dry gin
½ jigger lemon juice
1 tablespoon grenadine
1 egg white
Shake well and pour into chilled glass.

Pink Rose

⅔ jigger dry gin
1 teaspoon grenadine
1 teaspoon lemon juice
1 teaspoon cream
1 egg white
Shake well with ice and strain into glass.

Polly (Poppy)

⅔ dry gin
⅓ crème de cacao
Stir well with ice and strain into glass.

Pollyanna

1 jigger dry gin
¼ jigger grenadine
¼ jigger sweet vermouth
2 slices orange

½ slice pineapple
Mash the orange and pineapple slices in the bottom of a shaker. Add ice and the other ingredients. Shake well and strain into glass.

Polo

⅔ dry gin
⅙ grapefruit juice
⅙ orange juice
Shake well with ice and strain into glass.

Pooh-Bah

⅓ dry gin
⅓ light rum
⅓ Swedish punsch
1 dash apricot brandy
Stir well with ice and strain into glass.

Princess Mary

⅓ dry gin
⅓ crème de cacao
⅓ cream
Shake well with ice and strain into glass.

Prince's Smile

½ dry gin
¼ calvados or apple brandy
¼ apricot brandy
1 dash lemon juice
Stir well with ice and strain into glass.

Princeton

1 jigger dry gin
⅓ jigger port
2 dashes orange bitters
Stir with ice and strain into glass. Serve with a twist of lemon peel.

Queen

⅔ dry gin
⅓ sweet vermouth
2 slices pineapple
Mash pineapple slices in shaker.
Add other ingredients with ice.
Stir well and strain into glass.

Queen Elizabeth (Gin)

½ dry gin
¼ Cointreau
¼ lemon juice
1 dash Pernod
Stir well with ice and strain into
glass. (See Index.)

Racquet Club

⅔ dry gin
⅓ dry vermouth
1 dash orange bitters
Stir well with ice and strain into
glass.

Resolute

½ dry gin
¼ apricot brandy
¼ lemon juice
Stir well with ice and strain into
glass.

Retreat from Moscow

½ dry gin
¼ kümmel
¼ lemon juice
Shake well with ice and strain
into glass.

Richmond

⅔ dry gin
⅓ Lillet
Stir well with ice and strain into
glass. Squeeze lemon peel over
top.

Roc-A-Coe

½ dry gin
½ dry sherry
Stir well with ice and strain into
glass. Serve with a cherry.

Rolls-Royce

½ dry gin
¼ dry vermouth
¼ sweet vermouth
1 or 2 dashes Bénédictine
Stir well with ice and strain into
glass.

Rose No. 1 (English)

½ dry gin
¼ dry vermouth
¼ apricot brandy
4 dashes grenadine
1 dash lemon juice
Shake well with ice and strain
into glass. Frost rim of glass with
powdered sugar. (See Index.)

Rose No. 2 (French)

½ dry gin
¼ dry vermouth
¼ cherry brandy
Stir well with ice and strain into
glass. (Kirsch may be used instead of the dry vermouth. See
Index.)

Royal

⅓ dry gin
⅓ dry vermouth
⅓ cherry brandy
Stir well with ice and strain into
glass.

Royal Smile
½ dry gin
½ grenadine
2 dashes lemon juice
Stir well with ice and strain into glass.

Russian
⅓ dry gin
⅓ vodka
⅓ crème de cacao
Stir well with ice and strain into glass.

Sandmartin
½ dry gin
½ sweet vermouth
1 teaspoon green Chartreuse
Stir well with ice and strain into glass.

Satan's Whiskers—Straight
⅖ dry gin
⅕ dry vermouth
⅕ sweet vermouth
⅕ orange juice
1 dash Grand Marnier
1 dash orange bitters
Stir well with ice and strain into glass.

Satan's Whiskers—Curled
Prepare same as SATAN'S WHIS-KERS—STRAIGHT, using curaçao instead of Grand Marnier.

Savoy Hotel Special
⅔ dry gin
⅓ dry vermouth
2 dashes grenadine
1 dash Pernod
Stir well with ice and strain into glass. Squeeze lemon peel over top.

Self-Starter
½ dry gin
⅜ Lillet
⅛ apricot brandy
2 dashes Pernod
Stir well with ice and strain into glass.

Sensation
¾ dry gin
¼ lemon juice
3 dashes maraschino
3 sprigs fresh mint
Shake well with ice and strain into glass.

Seventh Heaven
½ dry gin
½ Dubonnet
2 dashes maraschino
1 dash Angostura bitters
Stir well with ice and strain into glass. Squeeze orange peel on top. Serve with a cherry.

Shriner
½ jigger sloe gin
½ jigger brandy
2 dashes sugar syrup
2 dashes Peychaud's bitters
Stir well with ice and strain into glass. Serve with a twist of lemon peel.

Silver
½ dry gin
½ dry vermouth
2 dashes orange bitters
2 dashes maraschino
Stir well with ice and strain into glass. Serve with twist of lemon peel.

Silver Bullet

½ dry gin
¼ kümmel
¼ lemon juice
Stir well with ice and strain into glass.

Silver Stallion

½ dry gin
½ vanilla ice cream
Juice of ½ lime
Juice of ½ lemon
Shake with small amount of shaved ice. Strain into tall glass and fill with club soda.

Silver Streak

½ dry gin
½ kümmel
Stir well with ice and strain into glass.

Sloeberry

2 jiggers sloe gin
1 dash orange bitters
1 dash Angostura bitters
Stir well with ice and strain into glass.

Smiler

½ dry gin
¼ dry vermouth
¼ sweet vermouth
1 dash Angostura bitters
1 dash orange bitters
Stir well with ice and strain into glass.

Snicker

⅔ dry gin
⅓ dry vermouth
2 dashes maraschino
1 dash orange bitters

1 teaspoon sugar syrup
1 egg white
Shake well with ice and strain into glass.

Snowball

½ dry gin
⅛ crème de menthe
⅛ anisette
⅛ cream
Shake well with ice and strain into glass.

Some Moth

⅔ dry gin
⅓ dry vermouth
2 dashes Pernod
Shake well with ice and strain into glass. Serve with a pickled pearl onion.

Sonza's Wilson

½ dry gin
½ cherry brandy
4 dashes lemon or lime juice
4 dashes grenadine
Stir well with ice and strain into glass.

So-So

⅓ dry gin
⅓ sweet vermouth
⅙ calvados or apple brandy
⅙ grenadine
Stir well with ice and strain into glass.

Southern Gin

2 jiggers dry gin
2 dashes orange bitters
2 dashes curaçao
Shake well with ice and strain into glass. Serve with twist of lemon peel.

Southside (Gin)
2 jiggers dry gin
Juice of ½ lemon
½ tablespoon powdered sugar
2 sprigs fresh mint
Shake well with ice and strain into glass. Add a dash of club soda if desired. (See Index.)

Spencer
⅔ dry gin
⅓ apricot brandy
1 dash orange juice
1 dash Angostura bitters
Stir well with ice and strain into glass. Squeeze orange peel over top and serve with a cherry.

Spring (for 6)
6 jiggers dry gin
2 jiggers quinquina
2 jiggers Bénédictine
1 dash bitters
Shake well with ice and strain into glasses. Serve with an olive.

Spring Feeling
½ dry gin
¼ green Chartreuse
¼ lemon juice
Stir well with ice and strain into glass.

Star No. 2
½ dry gin
½ calvados or apple brandy
1 dash dry vermouth
1 dash sweet vermouth
1 teaspoon grapefruit juice
Stir well with ice and strain into glass.

Stinger (Gin)
⅔ dry gin
⅓ white crème de menthe
Shake well with shaved ice and strain into glass.

Straight Law
⅓ dry gin
⅔ dry sherry
Shake well with ice and strain into glass.

Strike's Off
½ gin
¼ Swedish punsch
¼ lemon juice
Stir well with ice and strain into glass.

Sweet Patootie
½ dry gin
¼ Cointreau
¼ orange juice
Stir well with ice and strain into glass.

Tango
½ dry gin
¼ sweet vermouth
¼ dry vermouth
2 dashes curaçao
Juice of ¼ orange
Stir well with ice and strain into glass.

Thunderclap
⅓ dry gin
⅓ American whiskey
⅓ brandy
Shake well with ice and strain into glass. Drink this at your own risk!

Tidbit

½ dry gin
½ vanilla ice cream
1 dash sherry
Shake well till thoroughly blended. If you think anything else is necessary, serve with a cherry.

Transvaal

½ dry gin
½ Dubonnet
3 dashes orange bitters
Stir well with ice and strain into glass.

Trinity

⅓ dry gin
⅓ dry vermouth
⅓ sweet vermouth
Stir well with ice and strain into glass.

Tuxedo

½ dry gin
½ dry vermouth
2 dashes orange bitters
1 dash Pernod
1 dash maraschino
Stir well with ice and strain into glass. Add a cherry and squeeze lemon peel over the top.

Twin Six

1 jigger dry gin
½ jigger sweet vermouth
1 dash grenadine
2 slices orange
1 egg white
Crush orange in shaker. Add other ingredients. Shake well with ice and strain into glass.

Ulanda

⅔ dry gin
⅓ Cointreau
1 dash Pernod
Stir well with ice and strain into glass.

Union Jack

⅔ dry gin
⅓ Crème Yvette
Stir well with ice and strain into glass.

Van

⅔ dry gin
⅓ dry vermouth
2 dashes Grand Marnier
Stir well with ice and strain into glass.

Vie Rose

⅓ dry gin
⅓ kirsch
⅙ lemon juice
⅙ grenadine
Shake well with ice and strain into glass.

Virgin

⅓ dry gin
⅓ Forbidden Fruit
⅓ white crème de menthe
Stir well with ice and strain into glass.

Wardays

⅓ dry gin
⅓ sweet vermouth
⅓ calvados or apple brandy
1 teaspoon yellow Chartreuse
Shake well with ice and strain into glass.

Ward Eight No. 1
Prepare same as MARTINI (DRY), adding 2 twists of orange peel instead of lemon peel or olive. (See Index.)

Wax
2 jiggers dry gin
3 dashes orange bitters
Stir well with ice and strain into glass.

Wedding Belle
⅓ dry gin
⅓ Dubonnet
⅙ orange juice
⅙ cherry brandy
Shake well with ice and strain into glass.

Welcome Stranger
⅙ dry gin
⅙ Swedish punsch
⅙ brandy
⅙ grenadine
⅙ lemon juice
⅙ orange juice
Shake well with ice and strain into glass.

Wellington
1 jigger dry gin
2 dashes Swedish punsch
2 dashes cherry brandy
Juice of ½ lime
Stir well with ice and strain into glass.

Wembly No. 1
⅔ dry gin
⅓ dry vermouth
2–3 dashes calvados or apple brandy

Stir well with ice and strain into glass. (See Index.)

Westbrook
⅗ dry gin
⅕ sweet vermouth
⅕ Bourbon whiskey
½ teaspoon powdered sugar
Shake well with ice and strain into glass.

White
2 jiggers dry gin
2 teaspoons anisette
2 dashes orange bitters
Stir well with ice and strain into glass. Squeeze lemon peel over top.

White Cargo
½ dry gin
½ vanilla ice cream
Shake together till blended and pour into glass.

White Lady
½ dry gin
¼ Cointreau
¼ lemon juice
Shake well with ice and strain into glass.

White Lily
⅓ dry gin
⅓ light rum
⅓ Cointreau
1 dash Pernod
Stir well with ice and strain into glass.

White Rose
1 jigger dry gin
Juice of ¼ orange
Juice of 1 lime
½ jigger maraschino
1 egg white
Shake well with ice and strain into glass.

Whizz-Doodle
¼ dry gin
¼ crème de cacao
¼ Scotch whisky
¼ cream
Shake well with ice and strain into glass.

Wild Oat
¾ dry gin
¼ kirsch
1 dash lemon juice
1 dash apricot brandy
Shake well with ice and strain into glass.

Xanthia
⅓ dry gin
⅓ yellow Chartreuse
⅓ cherry brandy
Stir well with ice and strain into glass.

Yachting Club
⅔ Holland gin
⅓ dry vermouth
2 dashes sugar syrup
2 dashes Peychaud's bitters
1 dash Pernod
Stir well with ice and strain into glass.

Yale
1 jigger dry gin
½ jigger dry vermouth
3 dashes orange bitters
2 dashes sugar syrup
1 dash maraschino
Stir well with ice and strain into glass.

Yokohama
⅓ dry gin
⅙ vodka
⅓ orange juice
⅙ grenadine
1 dash Pernod
Stir well with ice and strain into glass.

Zaza
1 jigger dry gin
1 jigger Dubonnet
1 twist orange peel
Stir well with ice and strain into glass.

COCKTAILS—LIQUEUR BASES

[Note: Many of the following cocktails call for equal quantities of liqueurs. Hence their listing is arbitrary. Consult Index.]

AMARETTO

Amer-etto
1½ oz. amaretto
1½ oz. Bourbon or rye whiskey
Juice of ½ lemon
Shake well with ice and strain into glass. Serve with a cherry.

Amorous Amaretto
1½ oz. amaretto
1½ oz. orange juice
½ oz. Grand Marnier
Mix with ice in highball glass.
Fill with club soda.

Coconut Amaretto Sunrise
1½ oz. coconut amaretto
1 oz. tequila
3 oz. orange juice
Shake well with ice and strain into glass.

Stingaretto
2 oz. amaretto
1 oz. white crème de menthe
Shake well with ice and strain into glass.

Two Worlds
1½ oz. amaretto
1½ oz. white or golden rum
Serve over rocks with a slice of orange.

APRICOT BRANDY

After Supper
½ apricot brandy
½ curaçao
2 dashes lemon juice
Stir well with ice and strain into glass.

Apricot
½ apricot brandy
¼ orange juice
¼ lemon juice
1 dash dry gin
Shake well with ice and strain into glass.

Babbie's Special
⅔ apricot brandy
⅓ cream
1 dash dry gin
Shake well with ice and strain into glass.

Culross
⅓ apricot brandy
⅓ light rum
⅓ Lillet
Juice of ¼ lemon
Stir well with ice and strain into glass.

Ethel Duffy
⅓ apricot brandy
⅓ white crème de menthe
⅓ curaçao
Shake well with ice and strain into glass.

Festival
½ jigger apricot brandy
½ jigger crème de cacao
½ jigger cream
1 teaspoon grenadine
Shake well with ice and strain into glass.

Flag
Place a teaspoon of Crème Yvette in a cocktail glass. Shake with shaved ice 1 jigger apricot brandy and 4 dashes curaçao. Pour into glass carefully so as not to mix. Top with claret.

Havana
½ apricot brandy
¼ Swedish punsch
¼ dry gin
1 dash lemon juice
Stir well with ice and strain into glass.

Hop Toad
¾ apricot brandy
¼ lemon juice
Stir well with ice and strain into glass.

Mother Sherman
1½ jiggers apricot brandy
⅔ jigger orange juice
4 dashes orange bitters
Shake well with shaved ice and strain into glass.

Princess
¾ apricot brandy
¼ cream
Pour brandy into glass and top with cream so they do not mix. Serve after dinner.

Tempter
½ apricot brandy
½ port
Stir well with ice and strain into glass.

Tender
¼ apricot brandy
¼ apple brandy
½ dry gin
1 dash lemon juice
Shake well with ice and strain into glass.

Valencia
⅔ apricot brandy
⅓ orange juice
4 dashes orange bitters
Stir well with ice and strain into glass. (This may also be poured into a tall glass and filled with champagne.)

Yellow Parrot
⅓ apricot brandy
⅓ yellow Chartreuse
⅓ Pernod
Shake well with ice and strain into glass.

AQUAVIT

Aqua-Heering
1½ oz. aquavit
1 oz. Peter Heering cherry liqueur
2 teaspoons sugar
1 egg white
Juice of ½ lemon
Shake well with ice and pour into old-fashioned glass. Fill with club soda.

Cloudberry Conceit
2 oz. aquavit
1 egg white
1½ teaspoons cloudberry liqueur
Shake well with ice and strain into cocktail glass. (If cloudberry liqueur is unavailable, cranberry liqueur may be substituted.)

Copenhagen Mary
2 oz. aquavit
3 oz. tomato juice
1½ teaspoons lemon juice
1 dash Worcestershire sauce
1 dash Tabasco
Shake well with ice and strain into old-fashioned glass.

BÉNÉDICTINE

B. and B.
½ Bénédictine
½ brandy
Serve in a liqueur glass or iced in a cocktail glass. Serve after dinner.

Bénédictine
Place in a shaker with ice 2 jiggers Bénédictine and a dash of Angostura bitters. Shake slightly and strain into a cocktail glass, the rim of which has been rubbed with a slice of lemon and then dipped into powdered sugar. Serve with a cherry.

Bénédictine Frappé
Fill a large cocktail glass with shaved ice and fill with Bénédictine. Serve after dinner with straws.

Widow's Dream
2 jiggers Bénédictine
1 egg
1 jigger cream
Shake well with ice and strain into glass.

Windy Corner
2 jiggers blackberry brandy
Shake well with shaved ice and serve with a grating of nutmeg.

You Never Know
2 jiggers blackberry brandy
1 jigger white crème de menthe
1 grating of nutmeg
Stir well with ice and strain into glass.

French Summer
1 oz. Chambord
3 oz. Perrier or other sparkling water
Juice of ¼ lemon and ¼ orange
Stir with plenty of ice.

Montmartre
1½ oz. Chambord
1 oz. coffee liqueur
1 oz. cream
Shake with ice and strain into glass.

Chocolate (Chartreuse)
1 jigger yellow Chartreuse
1 jigger maraschino
½ jigger brandy
1 egg
1 teaspoon powdered sugar
Shake well with ice and strain into glass. (See Index.)

Golden Slipper
½ jigger yellow Chartreuse
½ jigger Danziger goldwasser
1 egg yolk
Shake well with ice and strain into glass.

Green Dragon No. 2
½ green Chartreuse
½ brandy
Stir with shaved ice and strain into glass. (See Index.)

H-Bomb
¼ yellow Chartreuse
¼ green Chartreuse
¼ brandy
¼ Bourbon whiskey
Shake well with ice and strain into glass.

Rainbow
⅐ yellow Chartreuse
⅐ green Chartreuse
⅐ crème de cacao
⅐ crème de violette
⅐ maraschino
⅐ Bénédictine
⅐ brandy
Pour ingredients carefully, in order listed, into large liqueur glass so that they do not mix. Serve after dinner. (This is a version of POUSSE CAFÉ; see Index.)

St. Germain
2 jiggers green Chartreuse
1 egg white
Juice of ½ lemon
Juice of ¼ grapefruit
Shake well with ice and strain
into large glass.

Stars and Stripes
⅓ green Chartreuse
⅓ maraschino
⅓ crème de cassis
Pour ingredients carefully, in
order listed, into liqueur glass so
that they do not mix. Serve after
dinner.

CHERRY BRANDY

Bulldog (Cherry Brandy)
1 jigger cherry brandy
½ jigger light rum
Juice of ½ lime
Shake well with ice and strain
into glass. (See Index.)

Merry Widow (Cherry Brandy)
½ cherry brandy
½ maraschino
Shake well with ice and strain
into glass. Serve with a cherry.
(See Index.)

Purple Bunny
1 jigger cherry brandy
⅓ jigger crème de cacao
⅔ jigger cream
Shake well with ice and strain
into glass.

COCORIBE

Beach Party (for 4)
1 cup CocoRibe
2 cups dry white wine
1 thin sliced orange
Mix well, with ice and serve in 4
glasses (or take along in ther-
mos).

Créme de CocoRibe (for 2)
½ cup CocoRibe
1 cup coffee ice cream
2 slices pineapple
Blend or shake well with crushed
ice. Strain into sherbet glasses.

Peach Colada
3 oz. CocoRibe
1 peach, peeled and sliced
Crushed ice
Blend or shake well with ice and
strain into glass. (If peach is
hard, mash.)

Piña Colada No. 1
2 oz. CocoRibe
2 oz. pineapple juice
Stir with plenty of crushed ice
and strain into glass.

Piña Colada No. 2
1½ oz. CocoRibe
2½ oz. light rum
1 tablespoon crushed pineapple
or 3 oz. pineapple juice
Shake with crushed ice and
strain into glass.

Strawberry Colada (for 2)

3 oz. CocoRibe
⅓ cup frozen sliced strawberries
1 oz. milk or cream
Shake well with crushed ice and
strain into glasses. Serve with a
fresh strawberry in each.

COINTREAU

Albertine

⅓ Cointreau
⅓ yellow Chartreuse
⅓ kirsch
1 dash maraschino
Shake well with ice and strain
into glass.

Blanche

⅓ Cointreau
⅓ anisette
⅓ white curaçao
Shake well with ice and strain
into glass.

Broadway Smile

⅓ Cointreau
⅓ Swedish punsch
⅓ crème de cassis
Pour ingredients carefully, in
order listed, into liqueur glass so
that they do not mix. Serve after
dinner.

Bud's Special

⅔ Cointreau
⅓ cream
1 dash Angostura bitters
Stir well with ice and strain into
glass.

Lollypop (for 4)

2 jiggers Cointreau
2 jiggers Chartreuse
2 jiggers kirsch
1 dash maraschino
Shake well with ice and strain
into glasses. Serve after dinner.

Sunrise

¼ Cointreau
¼ yellow Chartreuse
¼ crème de violette
¼ grenadine
Pour ingredients carefully, in
order listed, into liqueur glass so
that ingredients do not mix.
Serve after dinner.

CORDIAL MÉDOC

M. and B.

1½ oz. Cordial Médoc
1½ oz. Bénédictine
Stir in glass with or without ice.

Médoc Sour

1½ oz. Cordial Médoc
1½ teaspoons sugar
Juice of ½ lemon
Shake with ice and strain into
glass.

CRÈME DE CACAO

Angel's Kiss

¼ crème de cacao
¼ prunelle
¼ crème de violette
¼ sweet cream
Pour ingredients carefully, in
order listed, into glass so that
they do not mix. Best served
after dinner.

Angel's Tip
¾ crème de cacao
¼ cream
Pour carefully into glass, floating cream on top. Best served after dinner.

Angel's Wing
½ crème de cacao
½ prunelle
½ teaspoon sweet cream
Pour first ingredients carefully into glass so that they do not mix, and float cream on top. Best served after dinner.

Cola Cacao
2 oz. crème de cacao
½ oz. coffee-flavored brandy or liqueur
½ oz. cream
Blend or shake with ice and strain into tall glass. Fill with any cola drink.

Dutch Treat
1 oz. crème de cacao
1 oz. crème de banana
1 oz. strawberry liqueur
2 oz. cream
Blend or shake and strain into glass. Serve with a strawberry.

Golden Gopher
1 jigger white crème de cacao
1 jigger brandy
Stir well with ice and strain into glass.

Layer Cake
⅓ crème de cacao
⅓ apricot brandy
⅓ cream

Pour ingredients carefully, in order listed, into liqueur glass so that they do not mix. Place a cherry on top. Best served after dinner.

Mocha Cream (for 4)
1 cup crème de cacao
1 pint cold coffee
1 pint coffee ice cream
Stir liqueur and coffee with ice. Pour into tall glasses. Top each with ice cream.

Witching Eve
⅔ crème de cacao
1 dash Angostura bitters
⅓ cream
Pour ingredients carefully, in order listed, into liqueur glass so that they do not mix.

CRÈME DE GRAND MARNIER

[Note: This new liqueur from France may also be served neat or on-the-rocks.]

Creamy Gloom Chaser
¼ Crème de Grand Marnier
¼ Curaçao
¼ lemon juice
¼ grenadine
Shake well with ice and pour into an old-fashioned glass.

Crème de Grand Marnier and Coffee
Pour 2 oz. Crème de Grand Marnier into a coffee mug. Fill with hot coffee.

CRÈME DE MENTHE

Auf Wiedersehen
2 oz. white crème de menthe or peppermint schnapps
½ oz. Triple Sec or Cointreau
Stir and pour over ice.

Diana
½ white crème de menthe
½ brandy
Place ice in a glass and pour in crème de menthe. Top carefully with brandy.

Frappé (Crème de Menthe)
Fill cocktail glass with shaved ice. Pour in green or white crème de menthe.

Grasshopper
1 jigger green crème de menthe
1 jigger white crème de cacao
⅔ jigger cream
Shake well with ice and serve in champagne glass.

Pousse Café
⅙ grenadine
⅙ maraschino
⅙ green crème de menthe
⅙ crème de violette
⅙ Chartreuse
⅙ brandy
Add carefully, in order given, to keep each liqueur separate. (See Index.)

Stinger
See STINGER (BRANDY); also see Index.

CRÈME DE VIOLETTE

Angel's Wings
⅓ crème de violette
⅓ raspberry syrup
⅓ maraschino
Pour ingredients carefully, in order listed, into liqueur glass so that they do not mix.

CRÈME YVETTE

Lillian Waldorf
½ jigger Crème Yvette
½ jigger maraschino
Pour carefully, in order listed, into liqueur glass so that they do not mix and top with cream.

CURAÇAO

Baby's Own
⅔ white curaçao
⅓ cream
1 dash Angostura bitters
Shake well with ice and strain into glass.

Canadian No. 1
1 jigger curaçao
3 dashes Jamaica rum
1 teaspoon powdered sugar
Juice of ½ lemon
Shake well with ice and strain into glass. (See Index.)

Curaçao
⅓ curaçao
⅙ gin
⅙ brandy
⅓ orange juice

Shake well with ice and strain into glass with a dash of orange bitters.

Double Arrow
½ light curaçao
½ Crème Yvette
Pour carefully, in order listed, into liqueur glass so that they do not mix and top with cream.

Five Fifteen
⅓ curaçao
⅓ dry vermouth
⅓ cream
Shake well with ice and strain into glass.

DRAMBUIE

Highland Heather
1 oz. Drambuie
½ oz. sweet vermouth
½ oz. Scotch whisky
Stir well with ice and strain into glass.

Rusty Nail
1 oz. Drambuie
1 oz. Scotch whisky
Stir well with ice and strain into glass.

DUBONNET

Dubonapple
1½ oz. Dubonnet blanc
1 oz. calvados or applejack
1 dash Angostura bitters
Stir well with ice and strain into glass.

Dubon-Dubon
1½ oz. Dubonnet
1 oz. light rum
2 dashes Angostura bitters
Shake well with ice and strain into glass.

Dubonnet Blank
1 oz. Dubonnet blanc
½ oz. dry gin
½ oz. apricot brandy
1 dash lemon juice
Stir well with crushed ice and strain into glass. Garnish with a cherry.

FRANGELICO

Friar Tuck
4 oz. Frangelico
2 oz. lemon juice
1 teaspoon grenadine
Shake well with ice and strain into glass. Garnish with an orange slice.

Iced Tea Frangelico
2 oz. Frangelico
Strong tea, cooled
Orange slice
In a tall glass, with ice, pour Frangelico and tea to fill. Garnish with orange. Top with crème Frangelico (whipped cream flavored with Frangelico).

Merry Marco
2 oz. Frangelico
1 oz. white rum or Scotch whisky
Orange twist
Shake well with crushed ice and strain into glass.

Tropic

1½ oz. Frangelico
1½ oz. cream
1 oz. pineapple juice
Shake well with ice and strain
into wineglass. Garnish with a
twist of orange peel or a wedge
of pineapple.

GALLIANO

Gallibrando

1½ oz. Galliano
1 oz. brandy or grappa
1 oz. orange juice
Shake well with ice and strain
into glass. Garnish with a twist
of orange.

Harvey Wallbanger

For this most popular of all
drinks with Galliano, see below,
"Cocktails—Vodka Base."

Picca

1 oz. Galliano
½ oz. sweet vermouth
1 oz. American whiskey
Shake well with ice and strain
into glass. Garnish with a cherry
and a twist of orange.

Torpedo

1½ oz. Galliano
1 oz. amaretto
1 oz. heavy cream
Blend or shake well with ice and
strain into glass.

GRAND MARNIER

[See also listing above for
CRÈME DE GRAND MARNIER.]

Alfonso Special (Grand Marnier)

½ Grand Marnier
¼ dry vermouth
¼ dry gin
4 dashes sweet vermouth
1 dash Angostura bitters
Stir well with ice and strain into
glass. (See Index.)

Gloom Chaser

¼ Grand Marnier
¼ curaçao
¼ lemon juice
¼ grenadine
Stir well with ice and strain into
glass.

Red Lion

⅔ jigger Grand Marnier
⅔ jigger dry gin
⅓ jigger lemon juice
⅓ jigger orange juice
Shake well with ice and strain
into glass. Serve with a twist of
lemon or orange peel.

IRISH CREAMS

[Note: These comprise one of
the most amazing phenomena on
the spirits front. Out of nowhere,
they have leaped ahead to make
a significant contribution to the
current beverage scene. Irish
creams are a mixture of Irish
whiskeys, fresh Irish cream from

Irish cows, and a variety of honeys. How the manufacturers are able to use fresh cream and have it stay fresh in the bottle for long periods of time is an Irish secret. Serve them cold from the fridge or on the rocks. Mix them with coffee, vodka or Irish, Scotch, or Bourbon whiskey, for creamy new drinks. Or use them in cooking and baking. (The Italians, not to be outdone, have created a "Venetian cream" along similar lines.)]

Bog
1 oz. Irish cream
1 oz. Irish whiskey
4 oz. cold coffee
Stir well with ice and strain into old-fashioned glass. Top with whipped cream.

Irish-Italian
1½ oz. Irish cream
1 oz. Galliano
Stir well with ice and strain into glass.

IRISH MIST

Mist Sour
2 oz. Irish Mist
1 teaspoon sugar
½ oz. lemon juice
½ tablespoon water
Stir with ice and garnish with orange slice and a cherry.

O'Alexander
1 oz. Irish Mist
1 oz. crème de cacao
1 oz. cream

Shake well with ice and strain into glass. Sprinkle with nutmeg grating and garnish with a green cherry.

O'Kelly
1½ oz. Irish Mist
1½ oz. cognac or other brandy
3 oz. pineapple juice
Shake well with ice and strain into glass. Garnish with a green cherry.

ITALIAN CREAM

Gondo-Leer
1½ oz. Venetian Cream
1 oz. golden rum
Shake well with ice and strain into old-fashioned glass.

KAHLÚA

[Note: Any other coffee-flavored liqueur may be used instead of Kahlúa.]

Black Russian
See "Cocktails—Vodka Base."

Peanut Butter
1½ oz. Kahlúa
½ oz. tequila
1½ oz. cream
1 tablespoon creamy peanut butter
Blend well with ice and pour into glass.

Sunset
1 oz. Kahlúa
1 oz. golden rum
6 oz. orange juice
Stir in a tall glass, with ice.

LIQUEUR ESPRESSO

A demitasse can be given new interest with any one of a variety of liqueurs added to taste, including anisette, crème de menthe (white), kümmel, curaçao, Triple Sec, Cointreau, mandarine, Grand Marnier, or any coffee liqueur (Tia Maria, Kahlúa, etc.).

LOCHAN ORA

Golden Spike (Lochan Ora)
1½ oz. Lochan Ora
1½ oz. Scotch whisky
Pour over ice cubes in old-fashioned glass, stir, and spike with a twist of lemon. (See Index.)

Lochan Ora Golden Mist
2 oz. Lochan Ora
Pour over tightly packed shaved ice in an on-the-rocks glass.

LUXARDO

Gondoliere
1½ oz. Luxardo
2 oz. Scotch whisky
Serve on the rocks with lemon peel, as an after-dinner drink.

Luxardo Collins
2 oz. Luxardo
1½ oz. lemon juice
Stir with ice cubes in a tall glass and fill it up with any carbonated soft drink of your choice.

Luxardo Daiquiri
1½ oz. white rum
1½ oz. lemon juice
1½ oz. Luxardo
Shake well with ice and strain into glass. Garnish with a cherry.

MALIBU

Malibu and Coffee
1½ oz. Malibu
Hot Coffee
Stir well in an old-fashioned glass. Top with whipped cream, if desired.

Malibu Colada
1½ oz. Malibu
3 oz. pineapple juice
1 oz. milk
½ cup crushed ice
Shake well or use blender. Serve in a tall glass with pineapple slice.

Malibu-on-the-Rocks
Pour straight, over ice cubes, in an old-fashioned glass. Serve with a lemon twist.

Malibu Sunrise (for 12–15)
16 oz. Malibu
24 oz. orange juice
24 oz. grapefruit juice
4 oz. grenadine
Combine ingredients in a 3-quart pitcher, half filled with crushed ice. Add slices of two oranges. Serve in tall glasses with a cherry in each.

MARASCHINO

Knickerbein
1 jigger maraschino
1 jigger grenadine
1 jigger brandy
1 egg yolk
Shake well with ice and strain into glass.

MIDORI

Magpie
1½ oz. Midori
1 oz. vodka
½ oz. white crème de menthe
Blend with crushed ice and strain into glass.

Melonball
2 oz. Midori
1 oz. vodka
Pour over ice in a tall glass and fill with orange juice.

Midori Colada
2 oz. Midori
1½ oz. white or golden rum
4 oz. colada mix
Blend or shake with ice and strain into glass. Garnish with a cherry. (To make your own co lada, combine rum and coconut cream. Adding pineapple makes it a piña colada.)

Midori Cooler
Pour 2 oz. of Midori over ice in a tall glass. Fill with club soda.

Midori Margarita
1½ oz. Midori
1½ oz. tequila
1 oz. lime juice
Coat rim of cocktail glass with salt. Shake ingredients well and strain into glass without disturbing salt.

Universal 92
1 oz. Midori
½ oz. amaretto
1 oz. vodka
2 oz. pineapple juice
Shake well with ice and strain into glass. Garnish with a cherry.

MONIN

[Note: This new liqueur from France may also be served neat or on-the-rocks.]

Monin Pineorange
1½ oz. Monin
1 oz. pineapple juice
1 oz. orange juice
Mix with crushed ice. Strain into cocktail glass.

PISANG AMBON

Green Orange
⅓ pisang ambon
⅔ orange juice
Stir well with ice and strain into glass.

Pisang Pearl
⅓ pisang ambon
⅔ milk
Stir well with ice and strain into glass.

SABRA

Mediterranean Cream
2 oz. Sabra
1 oz. amaretto
1 oz. half-and-half or cream
Mix well with ice and strain into glass.

Sabra and Cranberry Juice
1½ oz. Sabra
3 oz. cranberry juice
Mix with ice and pour into glass.

Sabra and Cream
2 oz. Sabra
2 oz. half-and-half or cream
Mix with ice. Pour into small glass.

Sabra and Peppermint Schnapps
2 oz. Sabra
1 oz. peppermint schnapps
Mix well with ice and strain into glass.

SAMBUCA

Alla Mosca
1½ oz. Sambuca
5 coffee beans
Serve in a brandy snifter.

Appian Screwdriver
1 oz. Sambuca
1 oz. vodka
4 oz. orange juice
Shake well with ice and strain into glass. Garnish with a twist of lemon peel.

Manbuca
1½ oz. Sambuca
1 oz. Bourbon or American whiskey
½ oz. cream
½ egg white lightly whipped
Shake well with ice and strain into glass.

Roman Steppes
1½ oz. Sambuca
¾ oz. vodka
1 egg white lightly whipped
2 teaspoons Rose's sweetened lime juice
Blend or shake well with crushed ice and strain into glass. Garnish with a lime slice.

SLOE GIN

Ninety Miles
½ sloe gin
½ applejack
Shake well with ice and strain into glass.

Queen Bee
⅔ sloe gin
⅓ curaçao
1 dash anisette
Shake well with ice and strain into glass.

Sloe Gin No. 1
1½ jiggers sloe gin
½ jigger dry vermouth
Stir well with ice and strain into glass.

Sloe Gin No. 2
1½ jiggers sloe gin
2 dashes orange bitters
2 dashes Angostura bitters
Shake well with ice and strain
into glass.

White Man's Burden
1 jigger sloe gin
⅓ jigger apricot brandy
Juice of ½ lime
Shake well with ice and strain
into glass.

SOUTHERN COMFORT

Memphis Belle
Place ½ peach and a maraschino
cherry in a champagne glass.
Add shaved ice and fill with
Southern Comfort. Serve with
short straw and a small spoon.

Old-Fashioned (Southern Comfort)
Put 1 dash Angostura bitters in
old-fashioned glass. Add a twist
of lemon peel and ice cubes. Fill
with Southern Comfort as desired. (See Index.)

Rhett Butler
1 jigger Southern Comfort
Juice of ¼ lime
Juice of ¼ lemon
1 teaspoon curaçao
½ teaspoon powdered sugar
Shake well with ice and strain
into glass.

Scarlett O'Hara
1½ jiggers Southern Comfort
1½ jiggers cranberry juice
Juice of ¼ lime
Stir well with ice and strain into
glass.

Volcano
1 jigger Southern Comfort
⅔ jigger vodka
⅓ jigger light rum
Shake with cracked ice and
strain into glass.

STREGA

Eau de Vie de Strega
1½ oz. Strega
1 oz. brandy or grappa
1 teaspoon orange juice
Shake well with ice and strain
into glass. Garnish with a twist
of lemon peel.

TUACA

Caffè Italia
Add 1 jigger of Tuaca to hot
coffee. Add sugar to taste. Top
with whipped cream.

Lime-Osine
2 oz. Tuaca
Juice of 1 lime or ½ lemon
Mix with ice in a large glass. Fill
with tonic water.

White Tiger
2 oz. Tuaca
4 oz. cold milk
Mix well with ice in a tall glass.

COCKTAILS—NON-ALCOHOLIC

Basic Tea Punch (for 6–8)
2 cups strong hot tea
6 cups fruit juice
1 split ginger ale or club soda
Combine ingredients just before serving and sweeten to taste with sugar or syrup, etc. Pour over a block of ice in a punch bowl.

Black Cow
Fill a tall glass ¾ full of sarsaparilla and add 1 or 2 scoops of vanilla ice cream.

Black and Tan
Fill a tall glass, with 1 or 2 ice cubes, ⅔ full of cola. Fill up with milk. Stir and serve.

Clam Juice
Combine in a shaker 1 teaspoon tomato catsup, 1 pinch celery salt, 1 or 2 dashes Tabasco sauce, and ⅔ cup clam juice. Shake well with 1 or 2 ice cubes and strain into small tumbler.

Clam and Tomato Juice
Prepare same as CLAM JUICE, omitting catsup and using half clam juice and half tomato juice.

Club
1 lump sugar
2 dashes Angostura bitters
1 long twist lemon peel
Place sugar in old-fashioned glass and splash with bitters. Add other ingredients with ice cubes and fill with club soda.

Eggnog
1 egg
1 teaspoon sugar
1 pinch salt
¼ teaspoon vanilla
Milk
Beat egg with salt and sugar. Pour into tall glass, add vanilla, and fill with milk. Stir and sprinkle lightly with nutmeg.

Grape Juice Cup (for 10)
Place ice cubes in a large pitcher and add the juice of 6 lemons, 1 quart of grape juice and fill with club soda. Add grenadine to taste and decorate with fruit as desired. Stir and serve.

Horse's Neck (non-alcoholic)
Place rind of lemon in highball glass with ice and fill with ginger ale. (For alcoholic versions, see Index.)

Lemonade (for 4–6)
Juice of 6 lemons
1 quart water
1 cup sugar syrup or other sweetening
Combine ingredients in pitcher and chill. Pour over ice cubes in tall glasses. Garnish with fruit or mint as desired.

Orangeade (for 4–6)
Juice of 5 oranges
Juice of 1 lemon
½ cup sugar syrup
1 quart water

Prepare and serve same as
LEMONADE.

Parisette
Place in a tumbler several ice
cubes and 1 tablespoon grenadine. Fill with cold milk. Stir and
serve.

Pink Pearl (for 6)
1 cup grapefruit juice
2 teaspoons lemon juice
1 or 2 tablespoons grenadine
1 or 2 egg whites
Shake with crushed ice and
strain into cocktail glasses.

Prairie Oyster (non-alcoholic)
1 egg yolk
2 dashes vinegar
1 teaspoon Worcestershire sauce
1 dash Tabasco sauce
1 pinch salt
Slip egg yolk carefully into small
glass. Add seasoning. (See
Index.)

Rail Splitter
Juice of ½ lemon
⅔ jigger sugar syrup
Pour into glass with ice and fill
up with ginger beer.

Rosy Squash
Place in a tumbler with ice cubes
the juice of ½ lemon and 1 tablespoon grenadine. Fill up with
club soda.

Saratoga
Juice of ½ lemon
½ teaspoon powdered sugar
2 dashes Angostura bitters

Place ingredients in tall glass
with ice cubes and fill with ginger ale.

Sherbet Punch (for 8–10)
Place a large piece of ice in a
punch bowl and add 1 pint orange sherbet and 1 quart ginger
ale. (Break the sherbet into
chunks and pour the ginger ale
over it.) Decorate with mint
leaves and serve in punch cups.

Spiced Cider (for 4)
1 quart apple cider
¼ cup sugar
⅛ teaspoon salt
1 cinnamon stick, broken
12 whole cloves
8 whole allspice
Combine ingredients in a saucepan and bring to a boil. Cool
and let stand for several hours.
Strain and reheat before serving.

Spiced Lemonade (for 6–8)
1 cup sugar syrup
12 whole cloves
1 stick cinnamon
Juice of 6 lemons
1 quart water
Cook sugar, cloves, and cinnamon for 5 minutes. Add lemon
juice and let stand 1 hour. Add
water and strain into glasses over
crushed ice.

Summer Delight
Place 2 or 3 ice cubes in a large
tumbler. Add the juice of 1 lime
and ½ jigger raspberry syrup. Fill
up with club soda and decorate
with fruit as desired. Stir and
serve.

Summer Fizz (for 6–8)

12 sprigs mint
½ cup lemon juice
1 cup currant jelly
1 cup hot water
1 cup cold water
3 cups orange juice
1 pint ginger ale

Crush mint in a bowl and add boiling water and currant jelly. When jelly is melted, add cold water. Strain when cold into punch bowl. Add fruit juices and block of ice. Just before serving, pour in ginger ale and decorate with mint.

Temperance Cup (for 8–10)

Combine in punch bowl, with a block of ice, the juice of 4 oranges, the juice of 1 lemon, the juice of 5 limes, 3 tablespoons powdered sugar and 1 quart grape juice. Stir and decorate with fruit as desired.

Temperance Punch (for 15–20)

½ pound powdered sugar
1 quart cold tea
1 pint lemon juice
1 quart club soda
2 quarts white grape juice

Combine all ingredients in punch bowl with a block of ice. Stir and decorate with fruit as desired.

Virgin Mary

Combine in shaker with ice ⅔ cup tomato juice, juice of ¼ lemon, 1 pinch of salt, 1 teaspoon Worcestershire sauce. Shake well and strain into small tumbler.

COCKTAILS—RUM BASE

Apple Pie
½ light rum
½ sweet vermouth
4 dashes apricot brandy
4 dashes lemon juice
2 dashes grenadine
Shake well with ice and strain into glass.

Bacardi
2 jiggers Bacardi rum
Juice of ½ lime
2 dashes sugar syrup or grenadine
Shake well with ice and strain into glass.

Bacardi Special
⅔ Bacardi rum
⅓ dry gin
Juice of ½ lime
1 teaspoon grenadine
Shake well with ice and strain into glass.

Bahia
1 jigger light rum
1 jigger medium rum
1 jigger coconut cream
2 jiggers unsweetened pineapple juice
Shake hard with cracked ice or stir in blender. Strain into tall glass.

Beachcomber
1½ jiggers light rum
½ jigger Cointreau
Juice of ½ lime
2 dashes maraschino
Shake with shaved ice and strain into large cocktail glass.

Bee's Kiss
1 jigger golden rum
1 teaspoon honey
1 teaspoon cream
Shake well with ice and strain into glass.

Bolo

2 jiggers light rum
Juice of ½ lemon or lime
Juice of ¼ orange
1 teaspoon powdered sugar
Shake well with ice and strain
into glass.

Bombay (Rum)

2 jiggers dark rum
4 dashes lemon juice
Stir well with ice and strain into
glass. (See Index.)

Bushranger

½ light rum
½ Dubonnet
2 dashes Angostura bitters
Shake well with ice and strain
into glass.

Chinese

⅔ dark rum
⅓ grenadine
3 dashes curaçao
3 dashes maraschino
1 dash Angostura bitters
Stir well with ice and strain into
glass. Serve with cherry.

Columbia

1 jigger light rum
⅓ jigger raspberry syrup
⅓ lemon juice
Shake well with ice and strain
into glass.

Country Life

½ jigger dark rum
½ jigger port
1 jigger Bourbon whiskey
3 dashes Angostura bitters
1 dash orange bitters
Shake well with ice and strain
into glass.

Cuban No. 1

1½ jiggers light rum
½ jigger apricot brandy
Juice of ½ lime
Shake well with ice and strain
into glass. (See Index.)

Cuban No. 2

1 jigger light rum
1 jigger pineapple juice
1 teaspoon grenadine
1 teaspoon maraschino
Fill large glass with shaved ice
and pour in mixed ingredients.
Serve with straws. (See Index.)

Daiquiri

1½ jiggers light rum
Juice of ½ lime
1 teaspoon powdered sugar
Shake well with ice and strain
into glass.

Daiquiri (frozen)

2 jiggers light rum
1 tablespoon lime or lemon
juice
2 teaspoons powdered sugar
Place 2 cups shaved ice in a
blender. Add ingredients and
blend until consistency of snow.
Serve immediately with straw.
(Blended fresh or frozen fruit or
juices may be added to the
DAIQUIRI, as desired. Sometimes
a dash of maraschino and/or
grenadine is added.)

Daiquiri (banana)

Prepare the same as DAIQUIRI
(FROZEN), adding an inch piece
of banana.

Dunlop

⅔ light rum
⅓ sherry
1 dash Angostura bitters
Stir well with ice and strain into glass.

El Presidente

1 jigger light rum
⅓ jigger curaçao
⅓ jigger dry vermouth
1 dash grenadine
Shake well with ice and strain into glass.

Eyeopener

1 jigger light rum
2 dashes crème de noyau
2 dashes curaçao
2 dashes Pernod
1 teaspoon powdered sugar
1 egg yolk
Shake well with ice and strain into glass.

Fair and Warmer

⅔ light rum
⅓ sweet vermouth
2 dashes curaçao
Stir well with ice and strain into glass. Serve with twist of lemon peel.

Fireman's Sour

2 jiggers light rum
½ teaspoon powdered sugar
Juice of 1 lime
⅓ jigger grenadine
Shake well with ice and strain into Delmonico glass. Garnish with fruit if desired.

Flanagan

1 jigger dark rum
1 jigger sweet vermouth
½ teaspoon sugar syrup
1 dash Angostura bitters
Shake well with ice and strain into glass.

Florida Special No. 1

1 jigger light rum
1 teaspoon dry vermouth
1 teaspoon sweet vermouth
⅔ jigger unsweetened grapefruit juice
Stir with shaved ice and strain into glass. (See Index.)

Fluffy Ruffles

½ light rum
½ sweet vermouth
1 twist of lime or lemon peel
Stir well with ice and strain into glass.

Fog Cutter

2 jiggers medium rum
1 jigger brandy
½ jigger dry gin
2 jiggers lemon juice
1 jigger orange juice
½ jigger orgeat
½ jigger cream sherry
Shake all ingredients except sherry with cracked ice. Pour into large glass. Float sherry on top.

Four Flush

½ light rum
¼ Swedish punsch
¼ dry vermouth
1 dash grenadine or sugar syrup
Stir well with ice and strain into glass.

Governor's

Before your cocktail party place 1 vanilla bean in a bottle of light rum and leave it 24 hours. For your drinks, place 1 or 2 ice cubes in each champagne glass with 1 teaspoon sugar syrup and 1 twist lime peel. Fill up with rum.

Gradeal Special

½ light rum
¼ apricot brandy
¼ dry gin
Stir well with ice and strain into glass.

Havana Club

1 jigger medium rum
½ jigger dry vermouth
Stir well with ice and strain into glass.

Hawaiian

1 jigger dark rum
1 jigger unsweetened pineapple juice
1 egg white
1 dash orange bitters
Shake well with ice and strain into glass.

Honeybee

1½ jiggers light rum
⅓ jigger lemon juice
1 tablespoon honey
Shake well with ice and strain into glass.

Honeysuckle

1 jigger medium rum
Juice of ½ lime or lemon
1 teaspoon honey

Shake very well with ice and strain into glass.

Irish Elegance

⅘ jigger dark rum
⅕ jigger brandy
1 teaspoon crème de violette
⅓ jigger pineapple juice
½ teaspoon sugar
Juice of 1 lime
Mix in blender with shaved ice and serve immediately.

Jamaica Ginger

⅔ dark rum
⅓ grenadine
3 dashes maraschino
3 dashes curaçao
1 dash Angostura bitters
Shake well with ice and strain into glass.

Joburg

1 jigger light rum
1 jigger Dubonnet
4 dashes orange bitters
Stir well with ice and strain into glass. Serve with twist of lemon peel.

Kicker

⅔ light rum
⅓ calvados or apple brandy
2 dashes sweet vermouth
Stir well with ice and strain into glass.

Kingston No. 1

½ dark rum
¼ kümmel
¼ orange juice
Shake well with ice and strain into glass.

Kingston No. 2
1 jigger dark rum
½ jigger gin
Juice of ½ lime or lemon
1 teaspoon grenadine
Shake well with ice and strain into glass.

Knickerbocker Special
⅔ medium rum
⅓ curaçao
1 slice pineapple, crushed
1 teaspoon orange juice
1 teaspoon lemon juice
1 teaspoon raspberry syrup
Shake well with ice and strain into glass.

La Florida
1⅓ jiggers light rum
1 teaspoon sugar
1 teaspoon maraschino
Juice of ½ lemon
Shaved ice
Shake well and serve frappé, with a small straw.

Leilani
2 jiggers light rum
½ jigger lemon juice
½ jigger pineapple juice
½ jigger papaya juice
1 dash grenadine
Pour into large glass with ice. Stir and fill with club soda.

Little Princess
½ light rum
½ sweet vermouth
Stir well with ice and strain into glass.

Mai Tai
1 jigger dark or medium rum
Juice of 1 lime
½ jigger curaçao
1 dash sugar syrup
1 dollop orgeat
Shake hard with ice and pour into a tumbler.

Maragato Special
⅓ light rum
⅓ dry vermouth
⅓ sweet vermouth
1 dash kirsch
Juice of ½ lemon
Juice of ⅓ lime
½ teaspoon sugar, dissolved in water
Shake well with ice and strain into glass.

Mary Pickford
½ light rum
½ pineapple juice
1 teaspoon grenadine
1 dash maraschino
Stir well with ice and strain into glass.

Melba
½ jigger light rum
2 dashes Pernod
½ jigger Swedish punsch
Juice of ½ lime
2 dashes grenadine
Shake well with ice and strain into glass.

Miami
1 jigger light rum
½ jigger white crème de menthe
2 or 3 dashes lemon juice
Shake well with ice and strain into glass.

Miami Beach

1 jigger light rum
½ jigger Cointreau
1 dash lemon or lime juice
Shake well with ice and strain
into glass.

Naked Lady

½ light rum
½ sweet vermouth
4 dashes apricot brandy
2 dashes grenadine
4 dashes lemon juice
Shake well with ice and strain
into glass.

Nevada

1½ jiggers light rum
Juice of ½ grapefruit
Juice of 1 lime
1 dash Angostura bitters
1 teaspoon powdered sugar
Shake well with ice and strain
into glass.

Old-Fashioned (Rum)

Place 1 small lump sugar in old-
fashioned glass and sprinkle with
a few drops of Angostura or orange bitters. Add 1 large twist
lemon peel and fill glass with ice
cubes. Pour in medium rum as
desired and muddle. A slice of
lemon or orange or a cherry may
be added.

Olympia

1 jigger dark rum
⅔ jigger cherry brandy
Juice of ½ lime
Shake well with ice and strain
into glass.

Panama

1 jigger dark rum
½ jigger crème de cacao
½ jigger cream
Shake well with ice and strain
into glass.

Parisian Blonde

⅓ dark rum
⅓ curaçao
⅓ cream
Shake well with ice and strain
into glass.

Pauline

½ light rum
½ sweetened lemon juice
1 dash Pernod
1 grating of nutmeg
Shake well with ice and strain
into glass.

Pilgrim

1 jigger New England rum
1 teaspoon grenadine
Juice of ½ lime or lemon
Shake well with ice and strain
into glass.

Planter's No. 1

½ dark rum
½ orange juice
1 dash lemon juice
Shake well with ice and strain
into glass.

Planter's No. 2

½ dark rum
¼ lemon juice
¼ sugar syrup
Stir well with ice and strain into
glass.

Planter's Punch

[Note: There is no *one* way to make this drink. Each Caribbean island has its own version, usually made with its own rum.]
3 parts medium or dark rum
1 part lime juice
2 parts sugar syrup
3 parts water (including ice or club soda)
1 dash curaçao
1 dash Angostura bitters
Combine in a tall glass, stir, and garnish with cherries and an orange slice.

Platinum Blonde

2 jiggers light rum
1 jigger Cointreau
⅓ jigger cream
Shake well and strain into glass.

Quarter Deck No. 1

⅔ dark rum
⅓ sherry
1 teaspoon lime juice
Stir well with ice and strain into glass.

Quarter Deck No. 2

½ dark rum
¼ dry sherry
¼ Scotch whisky
1 teaspoon sugar syrup
1 dash orange bitters
Shake well with ice and strain into glass.

Royal Bermuda

2 oz. medium rum
Juice of 1 lime
Little sugar syrup
1 dash Cointreau
Shake with shaved ice and strain into glass.

Rum Dubonnet

½ jigger light rum
½ jigger Dubonnet
Juice of ½ lime
Stir well with ice and strain into glass.

Rum Frappé

Place 1 scoop orange or lemon sherbet in a champagne glass and cover with rum as desired. Stir and serve.

Rum Gimlet

4 parts medium rum
1 part Rose's unsweetened lime juice
Mix well over ice.

Rummy

1 oz. dark rum
1 oz. dry vermouth
½ oz. lime juice
½ oz. grenadine
Shake well with ice and strain into glass.

Rum Screwdriver

1 jigger medium rum
2 jiggers orange juice
Shake well with plenty of ice and strain into glass. (See Index.)

Rum Sour

2 jiggers dark rum
Juice of 1 lime
Sugar syrup to taste
Shake well with shaved ice and strain into Delmonico glass. Add slice of orange and cherry if desired.

Scorpion

2 jiggers light rum
1 jigger brandy
1½ jiggers lemon juice
2 jiggers orange juice
½ jigger orgeat
Use blender with plenty of ice
and strain into tall glass.

Sevilla No. 1

½ dark rum
½ sweet vermouth
1 twist orange peel
Stir well with ice and strain into
glass.

Sevilla No. 2

½ light rum
½ port
1 egg
½ teaspoon powdered sugar
Shake well with ice and strain
into glass.

Shanghai

1 jigger dark rum
⅔ oz. lemon juice
⅓ oz. anisette
2 dashes grenadine
Stir well with ice and strain into
glass.

Shark's Tooth

1 jigger light rum
½ jigger 151-proof rum
½ jigger lemon juice
½ jigger lime juice
1 dash sugar syrup
1 dash grenadine
Pour into large glass with ice.
Top with club soda.

Sonora

½ light rum
½ calvados or applejack
2 dashes apricot brandy
1 dash lemon juice
Stir well with ice and strain into
glass.

Suffering Bastard

2 jiggers dark rum
1 jigger light rum
Juice of 1 lime
¼ jigger curaçao
¼ jigger orgeat
Shake well with ice and strain
into glass. Serve with strip of cucumber rind. (Instead of the curaçao and orgeat, a ½ jigger of
Mai Tai mix may be used.)

Surprised (for 2)

2 jiggers Jamaica rum
1 jigger kümmel
1 jigger orange juice
Shake well with shaved ice and
strain into glasses.

Swing

⅓ light rum
⅓ Cointreau
⅓ dry gin
1 dash Pernod
Shake well with shaved ice and
strain into glass.

Tanglefoot

⅓ light rum
⅓ Swedish punsch
⅙ orange juice
⅙ lemon juice
Shake well with ice and strain
into glass.

Wedding Night
3 jiggers medium rum
½ jigger maple syrup
1 jigger lime juice
Shake with shaved ice and strain into champagne glass or flute.

West Indies
Prepare same as DAIQUIRI (FROZEN), adding pineapple juice to taste.

White Lion
1 jigger dark rum
Juice of ½ lemon
1 teaspoon powdered sugar
3 dashes Angostura bitters
3 dashes raspberry syrup
Shake well with ice and strain into glass.

XYZ
½ dark rum
¼ Cointreau
¼ lemon juice
Shake well with ice and strain into glass.

Yo Ho
⅓ medium rum
⅓ Swedish punsch
⅓ calvados or apple brandy
Shake well with ice and strain into glass. Serve with twist of lemon peel.

Zombie
1 jigger dark rum
1 jigger medium rum
1 jigger light rum
1 jigger pineapple juice
1 jigger papaya juice (optional)
Juice of 1 lime
1 teaspoon powdered sugar
Shake well with ice. Pour into tall glass. Garnish with pineapple and cherries. On top float a little medium rum.

COCKTAILS—TEQUILA BASE

Acapulco
1 jigger tequila
1 jigger Jamaica rum
2 jiggers pineapple juice
½ jigger grapefruit juice
Shake well with ice cubes and strain into glass.

Bertha
1 jigger tequila
Juice of ½ lime
1 dash grenadine
Shake with ice cubes. Pour into glass and fill with grapefruit juice.

Bloody Bull
1 jigger tequila
½ jigger lemon juice
1 dash Worcestershire
1 dash Tabasco
Mix with ice and strain into large glass. Fill with beef bouillon and tomato juice, half and half.

El Diablo
1 jigger tequila
Juice of ½ lime
½ jigger crème de cassis
Stir with ice in large glass. Fill with ginger ale.

Margarita (Grande)
1 jigger tequila
½ jigger Triple Sec or Cointreau
Juice of ½ lime
Coat rim of glass with salt by
moistening first. Stir ingredients
with ice and strain into glass.

Mexican Lover
1 jigger tequila
½ jigger brandy
½ jigger sweet vermouth
Stir well with ice and strain into
glass.

Picador
2 parts tequila
1 part Kahlúa or Tia Maria
Stir well with ice and strain into
glass.

Prado
1 jigger tequila
Juice of ½ lemon
A little egg white
1 dollop maraschino
1 dash grenadine
Shake vigorously with ice and
strain into glass.

Sangrita
1 jigger tequila
2 jiggers sangria
Stir well with ice and strain into
glass.

Tequila España
1 part tequila
1 part medium sherry
Chill with ice. Serve in wineglass.

Tequila Matador
1 jigger tequila
2 jiggers pineapple juice
Juice of ½ lime
Shake well with ice and strain
into glass.

Tequila
[Note: This is the original way
of drinking tequila.]
1 jigger tequila
1 wedge of lemon
1 pinch of salt
Put salt in notch of thumb and
forefinger of one hand; hold
lemon in same hand. In other
hand hold small glass with tequila. Now suck the lemon, take
a lick of salt, and swallow tequila.

Tequila Sunrise
1 jigger tequila
⅓ teaspoon crème de cassis
1 teaspoon grenadine
Juice of ½ lime
Stir everything with ice in tall
glass. Fill with club soda.

COCKTAILS—VODKA BASE

Barbara (Russian Bear)
½ vodka
¼ crème de cacao
¼ cream
Stir well with ice and strain into
glass.

Black Russian
1 jigger vodka
½ jigger Kahlúa
Shake or stir with ice and strain
into glass. (Made with Tia
Maria, the drink is sometimes
called BLACK CLOUD.)

Bloody Mary (Vodka)
1 jigger vodka
2 jiggers tomato juice
⅓ jigger lemon juice
1 dash Worcestershire sauce
Salt and pepper to taste
Shake well with ice and strain
into glass. (See Index.)

Blue Monday (Caucasian)
¾ vodka
¼ Cointreau
1 dash blue curaçao
Stir well with ice and strain into
glass.

Bullshot
1 jigger vodka
1 teaspoon lemon juice
1 dollop Worcestershire sauce
1 dash Tabasco sauce
Mix in large glass. Add ice. Fill
with chilled beef bouillon. (For
a BLOODY BULLSHOT, use half tomato juice and half bouillon.)

Cape Codder
1 jigger vodka
2 jiggers cranberry juice
Juice of ½ lime or ¼ lemon
Stir with ice cubes and strain
into glass. (If cranberry cordial
is used, this becomes a RED
RUSSIAN.)

Clam and Tomato
1 jigger vodka
2 jiggers clam juice
2 jiggers tomato juice
1 dash Tabasco
Stir over ice cubes in a tall glass.
(Clamato may be used instead of
the tomato and clam juice.)

Gazebo
1 jigger vodka
½ jigger apricot brandy
2 jiggers pineapple juice
2 dashes grenadine
Shake with ice. Serve in champagne flute.

Gimlet (Vodka)
1 jigger vodka
1 jigger Rose's unsweetened
lime juice
Stir with cracked ice in glass.
(See Index.)

Godmother
1 jigger vodka
1 jigger amaretto
Stir with cracked ice in glass.

Golden Spike (Golden Screw)
1 jigger vodka
3 jiggers orange juice
Shake with ice and strain into
glass or serve in tall glass with
ice cubes. (See Index.)

Harvey Wallbanger
1 jigger vodka
3 jiggers orange juice
½ jigger Galliano
In tall glass, with ice cubes, put
vodka, fill with orange juice, and
float Galliano on top.

Kangaroo
1 jigger vodka
½ jigger dry vermouth
Stir with cracked ice and strain
into glass. Serve with twist of
lemon peel.

Martini (Vodka)
4–5 parts vodka
1 part dry vermouth
Stir well with ice and strain into glass. Serve with a twist of lemon peel. (See Index.)

Moscow Mule
1 jigger vodka
Juice of 1 lime
Mix. Pour into mug with ice. Fill with ginger beer.

Russian
1 jigger vodka
1 jigger dry gin
1 jigger crème de cacao
Stir well with ice and strain into glass.

Salty Dog
1 jigger vodka
Pour into large glass with ice cubes. Fill with grapefruit juice.

Screwdriver
1 jigger vodka
Pour into large glass with ice cubes. Fill with orange juice.

Tovarich
1 jigger vodka
⅔ jigger kümmel
Juice of ½ lime
Shake well with cracked ice and strain into glass.

Vodka
1 jigger vodka
½ jigger cherry brandy
Juice of ½ lemon or 1 lime
Shake well with ice and strain into glass.

Vodka-on-the-Rocks
Fill an old-fashioned glass with ice cubes. Add vodka as desired and serve with a twist of lemon peel.

Vodka and Tonic
Pour 1 jigger vodka into a large glass with ice. Fill with tonic water.

Vodka and 7
Pour 1 jigger vodka into a large glass and fill with 7-Up.

Vodka Boatman
1 jigger vodka
1 jigger cherry brandy
1 jigger orange juice
Stir well with ice and strain into glass.

COCKTAILS—WHISKEY BASE

In the last edition of this work, whiskey cocktails were simply listed alphabetically, whether made from Irish, Scotch, or American. In this edition we list them by type of whiskey. Note that in the American category you will find subcategories such as rye, Bourbon, etc. That's for the purist; the rest of us use any American whiskey for any American drink.

It might be well to say a word about whiskeys in general at this juncture:

AMERICAN—Any whiskey born and bred in the United States.

Bourbon. By law, a whiskey made from over 50 percent corn, distilled at no more than 160 proof, and aged a minimum of two years in new charred oak barrels. It does *not* have to come from Bourbon County, Kentucky, or from Kentucky at all. In sweet mash Bourbon, fermentation is started by yeast; in sour mash, it is started by some of yesteryear's residue.

Rye. Defined by law the same as Bourbon except that it must be made from over 50 percent rye grain.

Corn. A whiskey made from at least 80 percent corn.

Whiskey. A general name that Uncle Sam gives to "an alcoholic distillate from the fermented mash of grains, distilled at less than 190 proof, and bottled at not less than 80 proof."

Blended whiskey. A blend of at least 20 percent 100-proof straight whiskey and 80 percent a combination of neutral spirits and/or other straight whiskeys. A majority of American whiskey is such a blend.

Bottled in bond. A term used for any straight American whiskey at least four years old, bottled at 100 proof, the product of a single distillery, and stored in government-controlled warehouses. It is tax-free until removed from the warehouse.

CANADIAN—A whisky produced in Canada from cereal grains by the distillation of fermented mash and aged from four to twelve years in wood casks. It is bottled at 70 proof in Canada or, if for export, at the proof required by the intended importer. In the United States that's 80 proof.

IRISH—Any whiskey made in the Republic of Ireland or in Northern Ireland.

Uisgue beatha, which means "water of life" in Irish Gaelic, is not too unlike Scotch in the making (see below). There was a time when all Irish whiskeys were pot-still malts. Today, just as with Scotch, Irish is a blend of pot-still malt and patent-still grain whiskey. The fact that Irish sprouted barley is not dried over open peat fires accounts for its lack of smokiness as compared to Scotch. Another difference is that it is three times distilled, Scotch only twice. Before Prohibition in the United States, it outsold Scotch hands down. Not so today. However, there is room for both these fine whiskeys on this side of the Atlantic.

JAPANESE—There is Japanese whiskey marketed in the United States. The makers, primarily Suntory, do not complain if it seems to resemble Scotch to the casual American palate.

SCOTCH—Any whisky made in Scotland.

Malt. A whisky made entirely of malted barley, the sprouted grain being dried over open peat fires which give the whisky its smoky taste. It is made only in pot stills. There are four types: Highland, Lowland, Campbeltown, and Islay.

Grain. A whisky made from any grains including corn (maize), wheat, oats, rye, etc. The patent, or continuous, still is usually used, not the pot.

Single malt. The product of one distillery, consisting of a single, unblended malt whisky, aged in oak casks (usually American oak) for varying lengths of time.

Blended Scotch. This is the Scotch whisky most commonly seen outside of Scotland. The great labels are all blends of malt and grain whiskies, usually in the proportion of 30–40 percent malt to 60–70 percent grain. (There is no requirement that the proportions be specified on the label.) It is bottled at U.S. 80 or 86 proof, seldom higher. It may be shipped in bulk and bottled in the intended country of entry. In the U.S., import taxes are figured on 100-proof spirits; hence it is advantageous to importers—and consumers, incidentally— to import the whisky in bulk, cut it with water to bottling strength, and pocket the taxes saved. The label must tell you where the product was made and bottled.

AMERICAN OR BLENDED

Horse's Neck (Whiskey)
1 jigger American whiskey
Rind of 1 entire lemon
1 dash of Angostura (optional)
Put into tall glass with ice. Fill
with pale ginger ale. (See
Index.)

New York
1½ jiggers American whiskey
1 dash grenadine
Juice of ½ lime
1 twist orange peel
½ teaspoon powdered sugar
Shake well with ice and strain
into glass.

Pick-Up
⅔ American whiskey
⅓ Fernet Branca
3 dashes Pernod
1 slice lemon
Stir gently with a little ice and
strain into glass.

Quaker
½ American whiskey
½ brandy
1 teaspoon raspberry syrup
Juice of ½ lime
Shake well with ice and strain
into glass.

Rattlesnake (for 6)
8 jiggers American whiskey
2 egg whites
2 jiggers sweetened lemon juice
3 dashes Pernod
Shake well with ice and strain
into glasses.

Russell House (Down the Hatch)
2 jiggers American whiskey
3 dashes blackberry brandy
2 dashes sugar syrup
2 dashes orange bitters
Stir well with ice and strain into
glass.

Sazerac
1 jigger American whiskey
1 dash Pernod
1 dash Peychaud's bitters
1 lump sugar dissolved in 1 teaspoon water
Stir well with ice and strain into
a chilled glass. Squeeze lemon
peel over top.

T.N.T.
½ American whiskey
½ Pernod
Shake well with ice and strain
into glass.

Ward Eight No. 2
1 jigger blended whiskey
Juice ¼ lemon or ½ lime
2 or 4 dashes grenadine
Dash orange bitters (optional)
Shake well with ice and strain
into goblet. Add extra ice and
fruit garnish as desired. Serve
with straws. (Rye or Bourbon
whiskey may be used instead of
blended whiskey. See Index.)

BOURBON

Bourbon Cola
Pour 1 jigger Bourbon whiskey
into tall glass and fill it up with
any cola drink.

Bourbon Mist

2 jiggers Bourbon whiskey
Fill old-fashioned glass with
shaved ice. Pour in whiskey.

Broken Leg

1 jigger Bourbon whiskey
3 jiggers hot cider or apple juice
4 or 5 raisins
Cinnamon stick or 1 shake of
cinnamon
Lemon slice
Pour all into serving mug.

Capetown

½ Bourbon or blended whiskey
½ Dubonnet
3 dashes curaçao
1 dash Angostura bitters
Stir well with ice and strain into
glass. Serve with twist of lemon
peel.

Dixie (for 6)

6 jiggers Bourbon whiskey
2 teaspoons sugar
2 dashes Angostura bitters
1 teaspoon lemon juice
1 teaspoon curaçao
2 teaspoons white crème de
menthe
Shake well with ice and strain
into glasses. Garnish with mint
leaves.

Edward VIII

Place in an old-fashioned glass 2
jiggers Bourbon whiskey, 1 dash
Pernod, and 2 teaspoons each
sweet vermouth and water. Add
1 or 2 ice cubes and twist of orange peel. Stir and serve.

Eggnog

1 jigger Bourbon whiskey
1 whole egg
1 tablespoon powdered sugar
1 glass milk or cream
Shake hard with ice and strain
into glass. Sprinkle a pinch of
nutmeg on top.

Elk's Own

½ Bourbon whiskey
½ port
1 egg white
Juice of ½ lemon
1 teaspoon sugar
Shake well with ice and strain
into glass. Serve with small
wedge of pineapple (optional).

Frisco

1 jigger Bourbon whiskey
½ jigger Bénédictine
Stir with shaved ice and strain
into glass. Serve with a twist of
lemon peel.

Grace's Delight (for 6)

4 jiggers Bourbon or blended
whiskey
5 jiggers dry vermouth
1 jigger framboise
Juice of ½ orange
1 teaspoon orange bitters
1 pinch cinnamon
1 pinch nutmeg
Combine all ingredients in
shaker and place on ice for 1
hour. Shake without ice and
strain into glasses.

Kentucky Colonel
1 jigger Bourbon whiskey
⅓ jigger Bénédictine
Stir with ice cubes in glass.

King Cole
1 jigger Bourbon whiskey
1 dash Fernet Branca
2 dashes sugar syrup
1 slice orange
1 slice pineapple
1 ice cube
Muddle all ingredients well in glass.

Manhattan (Perfect)
1 jigger Bourbon whiskey
⅓ jigger dry vermouth
⅓ jigger sweet vermouth
1 dash Angostura bitters (optional)
Stir well with ice and strain into glass. (See Index.)

Maple Leaf
1 jigger Bourbon whiskey
1 teaspoon maple syrup
Juice of ½ lemon
Stir well over ice in glass.

Millionaire
1 jigger Bourbon whiskey
⅓ jigger curaçao
1 egg white
1 dash grenadine
Shake well with shaved ice and strain into large cocktail glass.

New Orleans
1 jigger Bourbon whiskey
1 dash orange bitters
2 dashes Angostura bitters
1 dash anisette
2 dashes Pernod
½ lump sugar
Stir well with ice and strain into glass. Serve with twist of lemon peel.

Rah-Rah-Rut
1 jigger Bourbon whiskey
2 dashes Pernod
2 dashes Peychaud's bitters
Stir well with ice and strain into glass.

Sidecar (Bourbon)
1 jigger Bourbon whiskey
½ jigger Triple Sec or Cointreau
Juice of ½ lime
Shake well with cracked ice and strain into glass. (See Index.)

Southside (Bourbon)
Muddle in a mixing glass or shaker a few fresh mint leaves with 1 teaspoon powdered sugar. Add juice of ½ lemon and 1½ jiggers Bourbon whiskey. Shake thoroughly with ice and strain into glass. (See Index.)

S.S. Manhattan
½ Bourbon whiskey
½ orange juice
1 dash Bénédictine
Shake well with ice and strain into glass.

Stinger (Bourbon)
1 jigger Bourbon whiskey
⅔ jigger white crème de menthe
Shake well with cracked ice and strain into glass. (See Index.)

Waldorf No. 2

⅓ Bourbon whiskey
⅓ Pernod
⅓ sweet vermouth
3 dashes Angostura bitters
Stir well with ice and strain into
glass. (See Index.)

CORN

Corn Popper (for 6–8)

1 pint corn whiskey
1 cup cream
2 egg whites
1 tablespoon grenadine
Shake without ice and fill cocktail glasses ½ full. Add 1 ice cube
to each and fill with club soda.

RYE

Appetizer

2 jiggers rye whiskey
3 dashes curaçao
2 dashes Peychaud's bitters
1 twist each lemon and orange
peel
Shake well with ice and strain
into glass.

Blinker

1 jigger rye or blended whiskey
1½ jiggers grapefruit juice
½ jigger grenadine
Shake well with ice and strain
into glass.

Boomerang

⅓ rye whiskey
⅓ Swedish punsch
⅓ dry vermouth
1 dash Angostura bitters
1 dash lemon juice

Stir well with ice and strain into
glass.

Brooklyn

⅔ rye whiskey
⅓ dry vermouth
1 dash maraschino
1 dash Amer Picon
Stir well with ice and strain into
glass.

Commodore

2 jiggers rye whiskey
Juice of ½ lime or ¼ lemon
2 dashes orange bitters
1 teaspoon sugar syrup
Shake well with ice and strain
into glass.

Dandy

½ rye whiskey
½ Dubonnet
1 dash Angostura bitters
3 dashes Cointreau
1 twist each lemon and orange
peel
Stir well with ice and strain into
glass.

Deshler

1 jigger rye whiskey
1 jigger Dubonnet
2 dashes Peychaud's bitters
2 dashes Cointreau
2 twists orange peel
1 twist lemon peel
Shake well with ice and strain
into glass. Serve with a twist of
orange peel.

Evans
2 jiggers rye whiskey
1 dash apricot brandy
1 dash curaçao
Stir with ice and strain.

Flu
2 jiggers rye whiskey
1 teaspoon ginger brandy
1 teaspoon sugar syrup
1 dollop Jamaica rum
Juice of ¼ lemon
Stir well without ice and strain into glass. (This is supposedly a medicine.)

Hot Deck
¾ rye whiskey
¼ sweet vermouth
1 dash Jamaica ginger
Shake well with ice and strain into glass.

Hurricane
½ jigger rye or Bourbon whiskey
½ jigger white crème de menthe
½ jigger dry gin
Juice of 1 lemon
Shake well with ice and strain into glass.

Kitchen Sink
¼ rye whiskey
¼ dry gin
¼ lemon juice
¼ orange juice
1 egg
1 teaspoon apricot brandy
½ teaspoon powdered sugar
Shake well with ice and strain into glass.

Lawhill
⅔ rye whiskey
⅓ dry vermouth
1 dash Pernod
1 dash maraschino
1 dash Angostura bitters
Stir well with ice and strain into glass.

Master of the Hounds
1 jigger rye whiskey
⅓ jigger cherry brandy
2 dashes Angostura bitters
Stir well with ice and strain into glass.

Monte Carlo
1 jigger rye whiskey
⅓ jigger Bénédictine
2 dashes Angostura bitters
Shake well with ice and strain into glass.

Old Pal
⅓ rye whiskey
⅓ dry vermouth
⅓ Campari
Stir well with ice and strain into glass.

Old-Time Appetizer
½ jigger rye or Bourbon whiskey
½ jigger Dubonnet
2 dashes curaçao
2 dashes Pernod
1 slice orange
1 slice pineapple
1 twist lemon peel
1 dash Peychaud's bitters
Place all together in old-fashioned glass with ice cubes and serve with a muddler.

Rock and Rye

Dissolve 1 piece of rock candy in 2 jiggers of rye whiskey. Lemon juice may be added if desired. (Rock and rye also comes ready-bottled.)

Rye

2 jiggers rye whiskey
4 dashes sugar syrup
1 dash Angostura bitters
Stir well with ice and strain into glass. Serve with a cherry.

Soul Kiss No. 2

⅓ rye whiskey
⅓ dry vermouth
⅙ Dubonnet
⅙ orange juice
1 slice orange
Stir well with ice and strain into glass. (See Index.)

Temptation

1 jigger rye whiskey
2 dashes curaçao
2 dashes Pernod
2 dashes Dubonnet
1 twist each orange and lemon peel
Stir well with ice and strain into glass.

Up-to-Date

½ rye whiskey
½ sherry
2 dashes Angostura bitters
2 dashes Grand Marnier
Stir well with ice and strain into glass.

White Shadow

⅓ rye whiskey
⅓ Pernod
⅓ cream
1 pinch nutmeg
Shake well with shaved ice and strain into glass.

Yashmak

⅓ rye whiskey
⅓ Pernod
⅓ dry vermouth
1 dash Angostura bitters
1 or 2 pinches sugar
Stir well with ice and strain into glass.

Zazarac

⅓ rye whiskey
⅙ sugar syrup
⅙ anisette
⅙ light rum
⅙ Pernod
1 dash orange bitters
1 dash Angostura bitters
Shake well with ice and strain into glass. Squeeze lemon peel on top.

WHISKEY

Barney French

Place 1 slice orange, 2 dashes Peychaud's bitters, 1 twist lemon peel, and 1 or 2 ice cubes in an old-fashioned glass and muddle well. Add 1 or 2 jiggers whiskey and serve.

Boilermaker

Serve 1 large jigger of whiskey straight, with a beer chaser.

Choker (for 6)
8 jiggers whiskey
4 jiggers Pernod
1 dash bitters
Shake very well with shaved ice and strain into glasses.

Cowboy
⅔ whiskey
⅓ cream
Shake with shaved ice and strain into glass.

Derby (Oriental)
½ whiskey
¼ sweet vermouth
¼ white curaçao
Juice of ½ lime
Shake well with ice and strain into glass. Garnish with a mint leaf.

De Rigueur
½ whiskey
¼ grapefruit juice
¼ honey
Shake well with ice and strain into glass.

Duppy (Evening Gun) (for 5–6)
Pour 6 jiggers of whiskey into a mixing glass and add a few cloves. Let soak for about 1 hour. Add 5 or 6 drops orange bitters and 1 jigger curaçao. Shake well with ice and strain into glasses.

Earthquake
⅓ whiskey
⅓ gin
⅓ Pernod
Shake well with ice and strain into glass.

Evening Gun
See DUPPY.

Ladies'
1 jigger whiskey
2 dashes Pernod
3 dashes anisette
1 dash Angostura bitters
Stir well with ice and strain into glass. Serve with a piece of pineapple on top.

Linstead (for 6)
6 jiggers whiskey
6 jiggers sweetened pineapple juice
1 dash bitters
Shake well in ice and strain into glasses. Squeeze lemon peel over top.

Los Angeles (for 3–4)
4 jiggers whiskey
Juice of 1 lemon
4 teaspoons sugar
1 egg
1 dash sweet vermouth
Shake well with ice and strain into glasses.

Manhattan (dry)
4 parts whiskey
1 part dry vermouth
1 dash bitters
Stir very well with ice and strain into glass. Add a twist of lemon peel. (See Index.)

Manhattan (sweet)
⅔ whiskey
⅙ sweet vermouth
⅙ dry vermouth
1 dash bitters
Stir well with ice and strain into glass. Serve with a cherry. (See Index.)

Morning Glory
⅔ jigger whiskey
⅔ jigger brandy
1 dash Pernod
2 dashes bitters
2 dashes curaçao
3 dashes sugar syrup
1 twist lemon peel
Place ingredients in large cocktail glass, with 1–2 ice cubes. Stir and remove ice. Fill glass with club soda and stir with a teaspoon coated with powdered sugar.

Mud Pie
In an old-fashioned glass muddle ½ cube sugar with 2 dashes Peychaud's bitters, 4 dashes curaçao, and 1 large ice cube. Decorate with fruit, if desired, and serve with 1 jigger whiskey on the side.

Old-Fashioned (Whiskey)
Place in an old-fashioned glass 1 lump of sugar. Sprinkle it with a light dash of Angostura bitters. Add ice cubes and twist of lemon peel. (Add a cherry and orange slice, if desired.) Fill with whiskey. (See Index.)

Oh, Henry!
⅓ whiskey
⅓ Bénédictine
⅓ ginger ale
Stir well with ice and strain into glass.

Old Pepper
1⅓ jiggers whiskey
Juice of ½ lemon
1 teaspoon Worcestershire sauce
1 teaspoon chili sauce
2 dashes Angostura bitters
1 dash Tabasco sauce
Shake well with ice and serve in Delmonico glass.

Oriental
See DERBY.

Whiskey and Honey
Place in old-fashioned glass 1 teaspoon honey, 1 or 2 ice cubes, and 1 twist lemon peel. Pour in 1 or 2 jiggers whiskey. Serve with muddler and drink immediately.

Whiskey Sour
1 or 2 jiggers whiskey
Juice of ½ lemon
½ teaspoon sugar
Shake well with ice and serve in Delmonico glass, garnish with cherry and orange slice if desired. (The proportion of whiskey and sugar may be altered to suit individual taste.)

Whiskey Special (for 6)
6 jiggers whiskey
4 jiggers dry vermouth
1 jigger orange juice
1 pinch nutmeg

Shake well with ice and strain into glasses. Serve with a twist of orange peel.

CANADIAN

Canadian No. 2
1 jigger Canadian whisky
1 dash curaçao
2 dashes Angostura bitters
1 teaspoon powdered sugar
Shake well with ice and strain into glass. (See Index.)

IRISH

Blackthorn
½ Irish whiskey
½ dry vermouth
3 dashes Pernod
3 dashes Angostura bitters
Stir well with ice and strain into glass.

Bloody Molly
2 oz. Irish whiskey
2–3 oz. tomato juice
1 dash lemon juice
1 dash Tabasco sauce
1 dash Worcestershire sauce
½ teaspoon horseradish (optional)
Pour over ice in tall glass.

Brainstorm
2 jiggers Irish whiskey
2 dashes dry vermouth
2 dashes Bénédictine
1 twist orange peel
Place ingredients in old-fashioned glass with ice cubes.

Everybody's Irish
1 jigger Irish whiskey
6 dashes green Chartreuse
3 dashes green crème de menthe
Stir well with ice and strain into glass. Serve with a green olive.

Irish
1 jigger Irish whiskey
2 dashes Pernod
2 dashes curaçao
1 dash maraschino
1 dash Angostura bitters
Stir well with ice and strain.
Squeeze orange peel on top.

Irish Coffee
Into a large stemmed glass pour 2–3 oz. Irish whiskey, 3 oz. hot strong black coffee, and sugar to taste. Pour cream over back of spoon to float on top.

Irish Rover
1 jigger Irish whiskey
1 jigger Campari
2 jiggers orange juice
Dash grenadine
Serve on the rocks.

Irish Sour
1½ oz. Irish whiskey
Juice of ½ lemon
1 teaspoon sugar
Shake with ice and strain into glass.

John Wood
See SERPENT'S TOOTH.

Paddy
½ Irish whiskey
½ sweet vermouth

1 dash Angostura bitters
Stir well with ice and strain into
glass.

Serpent's Tooth (John Wood)
2 parts Irish whiskey
4 parts sweet vermouth
2 parts lemon juice
1 part kümmel
1 dash Angostura bitters
Stir well with ice and strain into
glass.

Shamrock (Friendly Sons of St. Patrick)
½ Irish whiskey
½ dry vermouth
3 dashes green Chartreuse
3 dashes green crème de menthe
Stir well with ice and strain into
glass. Serve with a green olive.

Tipperary
⅓ Irish whiskey
⅓ Chartreuse
⅓ sweet vermouth
Stir well with ice and strain into
glass.

Tom Moore
⅔ Irish whiskey
⅓ sweet vermouth
1 dash Angostura bitters
Stir well with ice and strain into
glass.

Wild-Eyed Rose
2 jiggers Irish whiskey
½ jigger grenadine
Juice of ½ lime
Place ingredients in large cocktail glass with 1 ice cube and fill
with club soda.

SCOTCH

Affinity (Perfect Rob Roy)
⅓ Scotch whisky
⅓ dry vermouth
⅓ sweet vermouth
2 dashes Angostura bitters
Stir well with ice and strain into
glass. Serve with a cherry and
twist of lemon peel over top of
glass.

Alice
⅓ Scotch whisky
⅓ kümmel
⅓ sweet vermouth
Stir well with ice and strain into
glass.

Automobile
⅓ Scotch whisky
⅓ dry gin
⅓ sweet vermouth
1 dash orange bitters
Stir well with ice and strain into
glass.

Blood and Sand
¼ Scotch whisky
¼ cherry brandy
¼ sweet vermouth
¼ orange juice
Stir well with ice and strain into
glass.

Bobby Burns
Prepare same as AFFINITY, adding a dash of Bénédictine.

Cameron's Kick

⅓ Scotch whisky
⅓ Irish whiskey
⅙ lemon juice
⅙ orgeat
Stir well with ice and strain into glass.

Continental

1 jigger Scotch whisky
⅔ jigger Kahlúa or Tia Maria
1 jigger milk
Stir over ice cubes in glass.

Fans

⅔ jigger Scotch whisky
⅓ jigger Cointreau
⅓ jigger unsweetened grapefruit juice
Shake well with ice and strain into glass.

Flying Scot (for 6)

6 jiggers Scotch whisky
4 jiggers sweet vermouth
1 tablespoon sugar syrup
1 tablespoon bitters
Shake well with ice and strain into glasses.

Godfather

1 jigger Scotch or Bourbon whiskey
⅔ jigger amaretto
Stir over ice cubes in glass.

Harry Lauder

½ Scotch whisky
½ sweet vermouth
2 dashes sugar syrup
Stir well with ice and strain into glass.

Highland Fling

1 jigger Scotch whisky
1 teaspoon sugar
2 jiggers milk
Shake very well with ice and strain into Delmonico glass.
Sprinkle nutmeg on top.

Hoots Mon

½ Scotch whisky
¼ Lillet
¼ sweet vermouth
Stir well with ice and strain into glass.

Loch Lomond

1 jigger Scotch whisky
3 dashes Angostura bitters
1 teaspoon sugar
Shake well with ice and strain into glass.

Mamie Taylor No. 1

1 jigger Scotch whisky
Juice of ½ lime
Pour over ice in tall glass. Fill with ginger ale or ginger beer.
(See Index.)

Mickie Walker

3 parts Scotch whisky
1 part sweet vermouth
1 dash lemon juice
1 dash grenadine
Shake well with ice and strain into glass.

Modern No. 2

2 jiggers Scotch whisky
1 dash lemon juice
1 dash Pernod
2 dashes Jamaica rum
1 dash orange bitters

Stir well with ice, strain into glass and serve with a cherry. (See Index.)

Perfect Rob Roy
See AFFINITY.

Polly's Special
½ Scotch whisky
¼ unsweetened grapefruit juice
¼ curaçao
Shake well with ice and strain into glass.

Rob Roy
1 jigger Scotch whisky
⅔ jigger sweet vermouth
2 dashes Angostura bitters
Stir well with ice and strain into glass. Serve with twist of lemon peel.

Rusty Nail
2 parts Scotch whisky
1 part Drambuie or Lochan Ora
Pour over ice cubes in an old-fashioned glass.

St. Nick's Coffee Cocktail
1 jigger Scotch whisky
⅔ jigger crème de cacao
1 teaspoon sugar
1 teaspoon instant coffee
2 jiggers cream
Stir well with ice and strain into cocktail glass.

Scotch Mist
Fill old-fashioned glass with shaved ice. Pour in Scotch whisky as desired. Add twist of lemon peel.

Scotch-on-the-Rocks
Fill old-fashioned glass with ice cubes. Pour in Scotch whisky as

desired, with or without water, and with or without twist of lemon peel.

Sidecar (Scotch)
1 jigger Scotch whisky
½ jigger Cointreau
½ jigger lemon juice
Shake well with ice and strain into large cocktail glass. (See Index.)

Thistle
½ Scotch whisky
½ sweet vermouth
2 dashes Angostura bitters
Stir well with ice and strain into glass.

Trilby
⅓ Scotch whisky
⅓ sweet vermouth
⅓ parfait amour
2 dashes orange bitters
2 dashes Pernod
Stir well with ice and strain into glass.

Wembley No. 2
⅓ Scotch whisky
⅓ dry vermouth
⅓ pineapple juice
Shake well with ice and strain into glass. (See Index.)

Whizz Bang
⅔ Scotch whisky
⅓ dry vermouth
2 dashes orange bitters
2 dashes grenadine
2 dashes Pernod
Stir well with ice and strain into glass.

COLLINS

The Collins is generally made in a highball glass. Its basic proportions are 2 or 3 cubes of ice, the juice of ½ or 1 lemon, 1 or 1½ teaspoons sugar, and 1 or 2 jiggers of any of the following liquors: applejack, brandy, gin, rum, whiskey, or vodka.

The proportions are a matter of personal taste, depending on the strength and sweetness of drink desired.

The TOM COLLINS uses dry gin. The JOHN COLLINS uses Holland gin.

COOLERS

Applejack Cooler
1 or 2 jiggers applejack
1 tablespoon sugar
Juice of ½ lemon
Shake well with cracked ice and strain into highball glass. Add ice cubes and fill with chilled club soda.

Apricot Cooler
1 jigger apricot brandy
Juice of ½ each lemon and lime
2 dashes grenadine
Shake well with cracked ice and strain into highball glass and fill with club soda.

Bishop's Cooler
Place in large highball glass 2 jiggers red burgundy, ½ jigger dark rum, ⅓ jigger orange juice, ⅓ jigger lemon juice, 1 teaspoon sugar, and 2 dashes Angostura bitters. Fill with shaved ice, stir, and serve.

Country Club Cooler
2 jiggers dry vermouth
1 teaspoon grenadine
Place in tall glass with ice and fill with chilled club soda.

Cuban Cooler
Place ice cubes in a tall highball glass and add 1 or 2 jiggers rum and fill with ginger ale. Garnish with twist of lemon peel.

Harvard Cooler
Place in a shaker with ice 1 tablespoon sugar syrup, juice of ½ lemon, and 1 or 2 jiggers applejack. Shake well and strain into tall highball glass. Fill with chilled club soda.

Hawaiian Cooler
Place ice cubes in a large tumbler or highball glass and add a long twist of orange peel, 1 or 2 jiggers rye whiskey and fill with chilled club soda.

Highland Cooler

Place ice cubes in a tall glass and add 2 jiggers Scotch whisky, 2 dashes Angostura bitters, juice of ½ lemon, and 1 teaspoon powdered sugar. Stir and fill with chilled ginger ale.

Irish Cooler

Place ice cubes in a large tumbler or highball glass with a long twist of lemon peel. Add 1 or 2 jiggers Irish whiskey and fill with club soda.

Long Tom Cooler

Prepare same as TOM COLLINS, adding 1 slice orange.

Manhattan Cooler

Place in a tall glass 2 or 3 jiggers claret, 3 dashes rum, juice of ½ lemon, and 1 or 2 teaspoons powdered sugar. Add ice and decorate with fruit if desired.

Mint Cooler

Place ice in highball glass and add 2 jiggers Scotch whisky, 3 dashes white crème de menthe, and fill with club soda.

Moonlight Cooler

2 or 3 jiggers calvados or applejack
Juice of 1 lemon
1½ teaspoons sugar
Shake well with shaved ice and strain into tall glass. Fill with chilled club soda. Decorate with fruit if desired.

Orange Blossom Cooler

Shake well with shaved ice 1 or 2 jiggers dry gin, juice of ½ orange, and 1 teaspoon sugar and strain into highball glass, filling with iced club soda. Garnish with fruit or mint.

Red Wine Cooler

Dissolve 2 teaspoons sugar in very little water and add 4 teaspoons orange juice. Pour into highball glass with ice cubes. Fill with any red wine and garnish with lemon slice.

Remsen Cooler

2 jiggers Scotch whisky
Rind of 1 lemon
Peel off lemon rind in as long a twist as possible and place in highball glass with ice. Add whisky and fill with club soda. (Dry gin may be used instead of Scotch.)

Scotch Cooler

Place in a highball glass 1 or 2 jiggers Scotch whisky, 3 dashes crème de menthe, and ice cubes. Fill with chilled club soda.

Sea Breeze Cooler

Place in a highball glass 1 jigger dry gin, 1 jigger apricot brandy, 1 dash grenadine, juice of ½ lemon, and ice cubes. Fill with chilled club soda and decorate with sprigs of mint.

Shady Grove Cooler
In a highball glass combine 2 jiggers dry gin, juice of ½ lemon, and 1½ teaspoons sugar. Add ice cubes and fill with ginger beer.

Stone Fence Cooler
Place 2 jiggers Scotch whisky and 2 dashes Peychaud's bitters in a highball glass with 1 small twist of lemon peel and ice cubes. Fill with club soda. (See Index.)

Whiskey Cooler
Place in a highball glass 2 jiggers rye or Bourbon whiskey, the juice of ½ lemon, 1 teaspoon sugar, and ice cubes. Fill with chilled ginger ale.

White Wine Cooler
Place 1 tablespoon sugar syrup and 2 or 3 jiggers chilled club soda in a highball glass with ice cubes. Fill with chilled white wine. Garnish with mint and, if desired, an orange slice.

Zenith Cooler
Place in a large tumbler several ice cubes with 1 tablespoon pineapple juice, 1 or 2 jiggers dry gin, and fill with club soda. Serve with a pineapple stick.

CRUSTAS

Crustas may be made with applejack, brandy, gin, rum, or whiskey. The following is the standard recipe: Rub the rim of a large wineglass with lemon, then dip glass in powdered sugar. Place in the glass a large twist of lemon or orange peel and a cherry. In a shaker with ice put 1 dash Angostura bitters, 1 teaspoon each lemon juice and maraschino and 1 or 2 jiggers of the desired liquor. Strain into prepared glass and serve.

CUPS

Burgundy Cup (for 10)
2 jiggers whiskey
1 jigger curaçao
1 jigger Bénédictine
1½ bottles red burgundy
1 pint club soda
4 tablespoons sugar
Place ingredients in large pitcher with ice cubes and stir. Decorate with slices of orange and pineapple, maraschino cherries, and cucumber rind.

Chablis Cup (for 8)
Place ice cubes in a large pitcher and add 1 jigger Bénédictine, 1 or 2 slices lemon, 3 thin slices pineapple, and 1 bottle chablis (or any other white burgundy). Stir gently and serve. (Peeled ripe peaches may be used in place of pineapple.)

Cider Cup No. 1 (for 6–8)
1 quart cider
1 jigger maraschino
1 jigger curaçao
1 jigger brandy
Place in pitcher with ice cubes and stir. Decorate with lemon or orange peel and serve in tall glasses.

Cider Cup No. 2 (for 4)
1 quart cider
1 jigger calvados
1 jigger brandy
1 jigger curaçao
1 pint club soda
Place all in pitcher with ice cubes and two large sprigs of mint. Stir and serve in tall glasses. (Apple brandy or apple-jack may be used instead of cal-vados.)

Claret Cup No. 1 (for 10)
1 bottle red bordeaux
½ jigger maraschino
½ jigger curaçao
1 jigger sugar syrup
Place in large pitcher with ice cubes and stir. Decorate with or-ange and pineapple. Add mint if desired.

Claret Cup No. 2 (10–12 cups)
Fill a large pitcher ½ full of cracked ice. Add 1 jigger cu-raçao, 1 jigger brandy, 1 jigger sugar syrup, 1 dash maraschino, 1 lemon sliced thin, 1 orange sliced thin, 2 or 3 slices fresh pineapple, and 1 or 2 bottles red bordeaux. Stir well. Add ½ pint club soda just before serving.

Cold Duck (Kalte Ente)
Place in a large pitcher whole curled rind of 1 lemon, 2 jiggers curaçao, 1 bottle chilled Moselle, and 1 bottle sparkling wine. Stir and serve.

Empire Peach Cup (15–20 cups)
Carefully peel 1 or 2 ripe peaches and slice into a large bowl or pitcher, losing as little juice as possible. Add 1 bottle Moselle and 2 or 3 tablespoons sugar. Stir and set aside, covered, for ½ hour. Add 1 more bottle Moselle and, just before serving, add ice and 1 bottle sparkling Moselle. (This cup is better if no ice is added and container is set in a bed of crushed ice.)

Grapefruit Cup (10–12 cups)
Place a large piece of ice in a bowl or pitcher and add 1 750-ml bottle brandy, 2 jiggers grenadine, and 1 quart can grapefruit juice. Stir and deco-rate with mint leaves. Just before serving, add 1 pint club soda.

May Wine Cup (25–30 cups)
In a large pitcher soak a bunch of woodruff in 3 bottles Moselle for 1 hour with a piece of ice. Add 6 lumps of sugar, 2 jiggers curaçao, 2 jiggers brandy, and 1 bottle sparkling wine before serving. (Bottled May wine is available these days.)

Moselle Cup (10–12 cups)
Place in a pitcher a large piece of ice, 3 peeled ripe peaches quartered, 12 maraschino cherries, 1 jigger Bénédictine, 1 bottle Moselle, and, just before serving, 1 ice-cold bottle sparkling wine.

Rhine Wine Cup (10–12 cups)
Place a large piece of ice in a pitcher or bowl, with slices of orange and pineapple, cucumber peel, and a few maraschino cherries. Add 1 jigger curaçao and 2 bottles Rhine wine.

Sauterne Cup (for 10–12)
Place a large bowl or pitcher in a bed of crushed ice. Combine the following ingredients in this order: 1 jigger brandy, 1 jigger curaçao, 1 jigger maraschino, 2 bottles chilled sauterne, ½ pint chilled club soda. Garnish with lemon and orange slices.

DAISIES

Daisies are overgrown cocktails. They should be served in very large cocktail glasses or goblets.

Place the juice of ½ lemon, 1 teaspoon grenadine, and 1 or 2 jiggers of applejack, brandy, gin, rum, or whiskey in a shaker with shaved ice. Shake well and strain into glass. Fill with chilled club soda. Sometimes the white of 1 egg and a dash of Pernod are added.

For a SANTA CRUZ RUM DAISY, fill a goblet ⅓ full of shaved ice and add 3 dashes sugar syrup, 3 dashes maraschino or curaçao, and juice of ½ lemon. Fill with rum. Stir.

FIXES

[Note: All fixes should be served in small tumblers with shaved ice and a straw.]

Brandy Fix
1 jigger brandy
1 jigger cherry brandy
1 teaspoon sugar
1 teaspoon water
Juice of ½ lemon
Moisten the sugar with the water and add the other ingredients. Fill glass with ice and stir gently. Add a slice of lemon or twist of peel.

Gin Fix
2 jiggers dry gin
1 teaspoon sugar
1 teaspoon water
Juice of ½ lemon
Moisten the sugar with the water

and add other ingredients. Fill with ice and stir gently. Add a slice of lemon or twist of peel. (Rum or whiskey may be used instead of gin to make a RUM FIX or WHISKEY FIX.)

Santa Cruz Fix
Prepare the same as BRANDY FIX, substituting rum for brandy.

FIZZES

[Note: Most fizzes are served in a 7-oz. highball glass.]

Alabama Fizz
Prepare same as GIN FIZZ, but adding a sprig of mint.

Albemarle
2 jiggers dry gin
½ tablespoon powdered sugar
1 dash raspberry syrup
Juice of ½ lemon
Shake well with ice and strain into glass. Fill with club soda.

American Fizz
1 jigger dry gin
1 jigger brandy
Juice of ½ lemon
1 teaspoon grenadine
Shake well with ice and strain into glass.

Apple Blow
2 jiggers applejack
4 dashes lemon juice
1 teaspoon sugar
1 egg white

Shake well with ice and strain into glass. Fill with club soda.

Bacardi Fizz
2 jiggers Bacardi rum
1 teaspoon sugar
Juice of ½ lemon
Shake well with ice and strain into glass. Fill with club soda.

Bismarck Fizz
See SLOE GIN FIZZ.

Boot Leg
Prepare same as GIN FIZZ, adding white of 1 egg and sprigs of mint.

Brandy Fizz
Prepare same as GIN FIZZ, using brandy instead of gin.

Bucks Fizz
1 jigger dry gin
½ teaspoon sugar
Juice of ½ orange
Shake well with ice and strain into glass. Fill with chilled champagne.

Cider Fizz (for 2)
2 jiggers golden rum
¼ cup apple cider
1 tablespoon lemon juice
1 teaspoon sugar
½ cup shaved ice
Prechill the ingredients and place them in glass container of electric blender. Cover and turn on for 20 seconds. Place two ice cubes in glasses. Pour in blended mixture and fill with club soda or ginger ale.

Cream Fizz
Prepare same as GIN FIZZ, adding 1 or 2 teaspoons cream.

Derby Fizz
1 jigger whiskey
5 dashes lemon juice
1 teaspoon sugar
1 egg
3 dashes curaçao
Shake well with ice and strain into glass. Fill up with club soda.

Diamond Fizz
1 jigger dry gin
½ teaspoon sugar
Juice of ½ lemon
Shake well with ice and strain into glass. Fill up with club soda.

Dubonnet Fizz
2 jiggers Dubonnet
1 teaspoon cherry brandy
Juice of ½ orange
Juice of ¼ lemon
Shake well with ice and strain into glass. Fill up with club soda.

Frank's Special Fizz
2 jiggers dry gin
¼ crushed peach
½ teaspoon sugar
Juice of ½ lemon
Shake well with ice and strain into glass. Fill with club soda or chilled champagne.

Gin Fizz
2 jiggers dry gin
1 tablespoon powdered sugar
Juice of ½ lemon
Juice of ½ lime
Shake well with ice and strain into glass. Fill up with club soda.

Golden Fizz
Prepare same as GIN FIZZ, adding yolk of 1 egg.

Grand Royal Fizz
Prepare same as GIN FIZZ, adding 1 dash maraschino, 3 dashes orange juice and ½ jigger cream.

Grenadine Fizz
2 jiggers dry gin
2 teaspoons grenadine
Juice of ½ lemon
Shake well with ice and strain into glass. Fill with club soda.

Hoffman House Fizz
2 jiggers dry gin
Juice of ½ lemon
1 teaspoon sugar
1 teaspoon cream
2 dashes maraschino
Shake well with ice and strain into glass. Fill with club soda.

Holland Gin Fizz

Prepare same as GIN FIZZ, using Holland instead of dry gin.

Imperial Fizz

1 jigger rye or Bourbon whiskey
Juice of ½ lemon
½ teaspoon sugar
Shake well with ice and strain into glass. Fill with chilled champagne.

Imperial Hotel Fizz

⅔ whiskey
⅓ light rum
4 dashes lemon juice
Juice of ½ lime
Shake well with ice and strain into glass. Fill with club soda.

Irish Fizz

2 jiggers Irish whiskey
1 teaspoon curaçao
½ teaspoon sugar
Juice of ½ lemon
Shake well with ice and strain into glass. Fill up with club soda.

Jubilee Fizz

½ dry gin
½ unsweetened pineapple juice
Shake well with ice and strain into glass. Fill with chilled champagne or other sparkling wine.

May Blossom Fizz

1 jigger Swedish punch
1 teaspoon grenadine
Juice of ½ lemon
Shake well with ice and strain into glass. Fill up with club soda.

Morning Glory Fizz

2 jiggers Scotch whisky
2 dashes Pernod
1 egg white
1 teaspoon powdered sugar
Juice of ½ lemon
Juice of ½ lime
Shake well with ice and strain into glass. Fill up with club soda.

New Orleans Fizz

2 jiggers dry gin
1 egg white
Juice of ½ lemon
1 teaspoon sugar
1 teaspoon cream
1 dash orange flower water
Shake well with ice and strain into glass. Fill with club soda.

Nicky's Fizz

2 jiggers dry gin
1 jigger sweetened grapefruit juice
Shake well with ice and strain into glass. Fill up with club soda.

Orange Fizz No. 1

2 jiggers dry gin
Juice of ½ orange
1 dash grenadine
Shake well with ice and strain into glass. Fill up with club soda.

Orange Fizz No. 2

2 jiggers dry gin
Juice of ½ orange
Juice of ½ lime
Juice of ¼ lemon
Shake well with ice and strain into glass. Fill up with club soda.

Ostend Fizz

1 jigger crème de cassis
1 jigger kirsch
Shake well with ice and strain into glass. Fill up with club soda.

Pineapple Fizz

2 jiggers light rum
½ tablespoon powdered sugar
2 tablespoons pineapple juice
1 dash lime juice
Shake well with ice and strain into glass. Fill up with club soda. (Dry gin may be used instead of rum.)

Ramoz (Ramos) Fizz

1½ jiggers dry gin
1 egg white
⅔ jigger cream
3 dashes orange flower water
Juice of ½ lime
Juice of ½ lemon
Shake well with ice and pour into 10-oz. glass with the edge frosted with lemon and sugar. Add club soda if desired.

Rose in June Fizz

1 jigger dry gin
1 jigger framboise
Juice of 1 orange
Juice of 2 limes
Shake well with ice and strain into glass. Add several dashes of club soda.

Royal Fizz

1 jigger dry gin
1 egg
1 teaspoon sugar
Juice of ½ lemon
Shake well with ice and strain into glass. Fill up with club soda.

Ruby Fizz

2 jiggers sloe gin
1 egg white
1 teaspoon raspberry syrup
Juice of ½ lemon
Shake well with ice and strain into glass. Fill up with club soda.

Rum Fizz

1 jigger rum
½ jigger cherry brandy
½ teaspoon sugar
Juice of ½ lemon
Shake well with ice and strain into glass. Fill up with club soda.

Safari Cooler

[Note: An African drink originally made with Waragi, an African-made gin.]
1 jigger dry gin
Lemon slice
1 dash Angostura bitters
Pour into large glass with cracked ice. Fill with ginger beer or ginger ale.

Saratoga Fizz

1 jigger rye or Bourbon whiskey
⅓ jigger lemon juice
1 teaspoon lime juice
1 teaspoon sugar
1 egg white
Shake well with ice and pour into glass. Garnish with a cherry.

Scotch Fizz

Prepare same as GIN FIZZ, using Scotch whisky in place of gin.

Seapea Fizz
2 jiggers Pernod
Juice of ½ lemon
Shake well with ice and strain
into glass. Fill up with club soda.

Silver Ball Fizz
2 jiggers Rhine wine
2 dashes orange flower water
1 teaspoon powdered sugar
1 egg white
1 jigger grapefruit juice
Shake well with ice and strain
into glass. Fill up with club soda.

Silver Fizz
Prepare same as GIN FIZZ, adding
white of 1 egg.

Sloe Gin Fizz (Bismarck Fizz)
2 jiggers sloe gin
Juice of ½ lemon
Shake well with ice and strain
into glass. Fill with club soda.

Southside Fizz
Prepare same as GIN FIZZ, adding
mint leaves.

Strawberry Fizz
1 jigger dry gin
4 crushed strawberries
½ teaspoon sugar
Juice of ½ lemon
Shake well with ice and strain
into glass. Fill up with club soda.

Texas Fizz
1 jigger dry gin
1 dash grenadine
Juice of ¼ orange
Juice of ¼ lemon
Shake well with ice and strain
into glass. Fill up with chilled
champagne.

Violet Fizz
1 jigger dry gin
1 teaspoon raspberry syrup
1 teaspoon cream
Juice of ½ lemon
Shake well with ice and strain
into glass. Fill up with club soda.

FLIPS

Applejack Flip (for 2)
2⅔ jiggers applejack
1 egg
2 teaspoons sugar
½ cup shaved ice
Chill all ingredients and place in
chilled container of electric
blender. Cover and blend for 20
seconds. Pour into 6-ounce
glasses and sprinkle with nutmeg.

Blackberry Flip
2 jiggers blackberry brandy
1 egg
1 teaspoon powdered sugar
Shake well with cracked ice and
strain into glass. Sprinkle nutmeg
on top.

Boston Flip
Place in a shaker 1 egg, 1 teaspoon sugar, 1 jigger madeira,

and 1 jigger rye whiskey. Shake well with ice and strain into large cocktail glass. Sprinkle with nutmeg.

Brandy Flip

Prepare same as BLACKBERRY FLIP, using straight brandy instead of blackberry brandy.

Cherry Brandy Flip

Prepare same as BLACKBERRY FLIP, using cherry brandy, instead of blackberry.

Claret Flip (for 2)

⅓ cup red bordeaux
1 egg
1 teaspoon sugar
1 dash Angostura bitters
½ cup shaved ice
Follow directions for preparation of APPLEJACK FLIP.

Muscatel Flip (for 2)

1⅓ jiggers brandy
¼ cup muscatel
1 egg
1 teaspoon sugar
1 tablespoon cream
½ cup shaved ice

Follow directions for preparation of APPLEJACK FLIP.

Port Flip

Prepare same as BLACKBERRY FLIP, using port instead of blackberry brandy and adding 1 or 2 dashes Bénédictine.

Rum Flip

Prepare same as BLACKBERRY FLIP, using golden rum, instead of blackberry brandy.

Sherry Flip

Prepare same as BLACKBERRY FLIP, using sweet sherry instead of blackberry brandy.

Whiskey Flip

Prepare same as BLACKBERRY FLIP, using any whisky instead of blackberry brandy and adding 2 or 3 dashes rum.

Whiskey Peppermint Flip

Prepare same as BLACKBERRY FLIP, using any whiskey instead of blackberry brandy and adding ½ jigger peppermint schnapps or crème de menthe.

FLOATS

Brandy Float

Place 1 or 2 ice cubes in an old-fashioned glass and fill it nearly full of chilled club soda. Lay the bowl of a teaspoon just at the top and pour in brandy carefully so that it flows out over the surface but does not mix. The amount of brandy is optional. Rum or any whiskey may be substituted for the brandy.

Liqueur Float
Fill a liqueur glass almost full of any liqueur you desire. Pour in cream carefully so that it floats on top.

FRAPPÉS

Frappés may be made in three ways and of any liquor or liqueur—or combination thereof—you desire.

1. Fill a cocktail glass with shaved ice and pour in the liquor. Serve with a straw.

2. Fill a shaker about half full of shaved ice, add the liquor, shake thoroughly, and strain into glass.

3. Blend shaved ice and liquor or liqueur together in an electric blender and pour unstrained into glass.

HOT DRINKS

Ale Flip (for 4)
Place 1 quart ale in a saucepan on the fire and let it come to a boil. Have ready the whites of 2 eggs and the yolks of 4, well beaten separately. Add them bit by bit to 4 tablespoons sugar which has been moistened with a little water and sprinkled with ½ teaspoon nutmeg in a bowl. When all are mixed, pour in the hot ale, beating as you do so. Then pour from the original bowl into another one backward and forward several times till the flip is smooth and frothy.

Apple Toddy
Place ¼ baked apple in a glass with 1 teaspoon powdered sugar and 2 jiggers calvados or applejack. Fill glass with boiling water and serve with grating of nutmeg.

Black Stripe
Place 1 teaspoon molasses in a heated tumbler with 2 jiggers dark rum and a twist of lemon peel. Add boiling water. Stir and serve.

Blue Blazer
This drink requires 2 good-sized mugs with handles. Put 2 jiggers Scotch whisky in one mug and 2 jiggers boiling water in the other. Blaze the Scotch and while it is blazing, pour the ingredients back and forth from one mug to the other. If you do this properly, it will look like a stream of fire. Add 1 teaspoon fine-grain sugar and serve in a heated tumbler with a twist of lemon peel.

Brandy Blazer
Combine in a small thick glass 2 jiggers brandy, 1 lump sugar, and 1 twist of orange peel. Blaze the brandy and stir with a long spoon. Strain into cocktail glass and serve.

Brandy Toddy
Dissolve 1 lump of sugar in a tumbler with a little water. Add 2 jiggers brandy and a twist of lemon peel. Fill with boiling water. Stir and serve.

Café Brûlot (for 6–8)
8 lumps sugar
6 jiggers cognac
2 sticks cinnamon, broken
1 twist lemon peel
12 whole cloves
2 large twists orange peel
5 demitasse cups of strong black coffee
Place all ingredients except coffee in a chafing dish. Heat gently, stirring constantly with a metal ladle until well warmed. Blaze and let burn about 1 minute. Slowly pour in the black coffee. Ladle into demitasse cups and serve.

Café Brûlot Cocktail
Moisten the edge of a heavy glass with a piece of lemon. Dip glass in powdered sugar and add about 3 jiggers hot coffee. Float ⅔ jigger brandy on top. Blaze and serve.

Café Diable (for 8–10)
2 cups bottled rock and rye
Rind of ½ lemon
Rind of ½ orange
4 cloves
2 lumps sugar
2 cups strong hot black coffee
Heat a silver or oven-proof glass bowl. Combine all ingredients except coffee in bowl. When

warm, ignite contents. Add coffee and stir until flame dies. Serve in demitasse cups.

Café Royale
2 teaspoons coffee liqueur
1 demitasse strong hot black coffee
1 lump sugar
Float 1 teaspoon of liqueur on hot coffee in demitasse cup. Put sugar on spoon and saturate with rest of liqueur. Ignite. Plunge while flaming into coffee. Stir and serve.

Christmas Punch No. 1 (for 30–40)
Combine in large kettle or heat-proof container 2 750-ml bottles brandy, 2 bottles champagne, 1 pound sugar, and 1 pound cubed fresh pineapple. Heat to a foam but do not boil. Pour ½ cup more of brandy on top and ignite. Let burn 1 minute and then ladle into wineglasses. (See Index.)

Columbia Skin
Heat in a small saucepan 1 tablespoon water, 2 lumps sugar, juice of ½ lemon, 1 teaspoon curaçao, and 2 jiggers rum. Let foam but do not boil. Serve in heated wineglass. (Brandy, gin, or whiskey may be used instead of rum.)

English Bishop (for 6–8)
Stick an orange generously with cloves and sprinkle it with brown sugar. Place it in a medium hot oven until moderately browned.

Quarter it and place it in a heavy saucepan with 1 quart of hot port. Simmer about 20 minutes and ladle into heated punch glasses. Add ½ jigger brandy to each glass before serving.

Farmer's Bishop (for 20)
1 bottle apple brandy
2 quarts apple cider
5 oranges stuck with cloves
Cinnamon sticks or ground cinnamon
Warm brandy and cider by immersing bottles in hot water. Do not boil. Roast oranges at 300° for 25 minutes. In *metal* punch bowl or pot put oranges and pour hot brandy over them. Ignite. Let burn just a few minutes (with dimmed lights to enjoy the spectacle). Then douse flame with hot cider. Pour into mugs or cups with a cinnamon stick stirrer in each or dust with ground cinnamon.

Festival Punch (for 20)
1 liter Jamaica rum
1 quart sweet apple cider
2 or 3 cinnamon sticks, broken
2 teaspoons ground allspice
1 or 2 tablespoons butter
Heat ingredients in a heavy saucepan until almost boiling. Serve hot in mugs.

Glögg (for 12)
6 jiggers red bordeaux
6 jiggers sherry
6 jiggers brandy
¾ cup granulated sugar
⅔ jigger Angostura bitters

Heat all ingredients in a heavy saucepan. Place spoons in heated old-fashioned glasses and pour ¾ full with the hot mixture.

Hot Benefactor
Place in a heated tumbler 2 lumps sugar dissolved with a little boiling water. Add 2 jiggers each Jamaica rum and burgundy. Fill with boiling water and serve with a slice of lemon and a grating of nutmeg.

Hot Buttered CocoRibe
½ cup CocoRibe
⅔ cup water
1 teaspoon brown sugar
2 teaspoons butter
1 2-inch cinnamon stick
1 pinch allspice
Combine water, sugar, 1 teaspoon butter, and cinnamon stick in saucepan. Bring to boil and simmer 2 minutes. Remove from heat. Remove cinnamon stick and stir in CocoRibe and allspice. Pour into mug. Melt other teaspoon butter on top.

Hot Buttered Rum
2 jiggers Jamaica rum
1 twist lemon peel
1 cinnamon stick
1 or 2 cloves
Boiling apple cider
1 pat butter
Place rum, lemon peel, clove, and cinnamon in a pewter tankard or heavy mug. Fill with boiling cider. Float butter on top and stir well.

Hot Gin
2 jiggers dry gin
1 or 2 lumps sugar
Juice of ½ lemon
Place ingredients in small tumbler and fill with hot water.
Serve with a spoon.

Hot Irish
3 oz. Irish whiskey
2 teaspoons sugar
1 slice lemon
4 cloves
1 pinch cinnamon
Mix well in glass tumbler. Put metal spoon in glass (to prevent breakage) and fill with boiling water.

Hot Lemonade
Prepare same as LEMONADE (PLAIN), using hot water instead of chilled club soda. Frequently 1 jigger whiskey, rum, or brandy is added. (See Index.)

Hot Locomotive
4 jiggers red burgundy or bordeaux
1 jigger curaçao
1 egg yolk
1½ teaspoons sugar
⅔ jigger honey
Blend egg yolk, sugar, and honey in small saucepan. Add wine and curaçao and heat to simmering point. Pour back and forth several times into a heated mug. Serve with a thin lemon slice and pinch of cinnamon.

Hot Milk Punch
1 jigger light rum
1 jigger brandy
1 teaspoon sugar
Hot milk
Combine the sugar, rum, and brandy in a tall glass. Fill with hot milk. Stir and top with nutmeg.

Hot Rum Bowl (for 16)
1 bottle Jamaica rum
3 quarts apple cider
1 cup brown sugar
1 cup boiling water
1–2 teaspoons butter
In a saucepan dissolve sugar in boiling water. Add cider and heat. Add rum and butter. Place in a heated bowl and sprinkle with nutmeg. Serve in mugs.

Hot Rye
In a small tumbler dissolve 1 lump sugar in little hot water. Add 1 small piece cinnamon, 1 twist lemon peel, and 2 jiggers rye whiskey. Serve hot water in a pitcher on the side, to be added as desired.

Hot Scotch
Prepare same as HOT RYE.

Hot Toddies
⅔ jigger applejack, brandy, rum, or whiskey
1 tcaspoon sugar
2 cloves
1 slice lemon
Place ingredients in old-fashioned glass with a silver spoon and fill with boiling water. A small piece of cinnamon may be added if desired.

Hot Toddy Bowl (for 16)
1 bottle applejack, brandy, rum, or any whiskey
2 quarts boiling water
1 whole lemon
Whole cloves
Sugar syrup to taste

Stud the lemon with cloves and slice it as thin as possible. Combine the liquor, sugar syrup to taste, and lemon slices in a heated bowl. Add the boiling water and serve in heated mugs with a lemon slice in each serving. Cinnamon may be added if desired.

Hot Wine Lemonade
1 jigger red wine
Juice of ½ or 1 lemon
1½ teaspoons sugar
1 twist lemon peel

Combine sugar, juice, and wine in a heated tumbler or mug. Add boiling water and twist of lemon peel.

Jersey Flamer (for 8)
1 bottle applejack
⅔ jigger Angostura bitters
1 cup sugar
2 large twists lemon peel
1 quart boiling water

Combine in saucepan the applejack, bitters, sugar, and lemon peel. Heat slightly and stir to dissolve the sugar. Turn into a heated heatproof bowl. Flame and pour on boiling water. Serve in heated mugs.

Jersey Mug
Place in a heated mug 2 jiggers applejack, 1 good dash Angostura bitters, several whole cloves, and large twist of lemon peel. Fill with boiling water and float applejack on top. Flame and serve.

Mariner's Grog
1 jigger Jamaica rum
1 lump sugar
Several cloves
1 small stick cinnamon
Juice of ½ lemon
1 slice lemon

Place all ingredients in a heavy mug. Fill with boiling water. Stir and serve.

Mulled Wine
2½ jiggers red wine
5 jiggers water
1 dash Angostura bitters
1 teaspoon sugar
1 large twist lemon peel
1 pinch ground allspice
1 small piece cinnamon
Several cloves

Heat ingredients together in a saucepan but do not boil. Place a silver spoon in a large tumbler and strain in the mixture.

(MULLED CIDER may be prepared the same way, using 7 jiggers cider instead of wine and water; a dash of rum may be added.)

Negus (8 cups)
Heat 1 bottle sherry or port in a pitcher. Rub a little lemon rind on 6 cubes of sugar and add to

the wine. Add 2–3 large twists of lemon rind and the juice of 1 lemon. Add 10 drops of vanilla and 2 cups of boiling water. Sweeten if desired and strain into glasses. Add a grating of nutmeg and serve.

Poet's Punch

1½ oz. Irish Mist
1 cup milk
1 egg yolk
½ teaspoon vanilla
1 stick cinnamon
1 twist each lemon peel and orange peel

Heat in a small saucepan everything except egg yolk to boiling point. Mix egg yolk with a little hot milk. Stir into drink. Serve in tall mug with a sprinkle of nutmeg.

Red and White (for 20–30)

1 bottle dry red wine
1 bottle dry white wine
½ gallon apple cider
½ teaspoon ground cinnamon
½ teaspoon whole cloves

Combine ingredients in a large pot and heat just to a boil. Serve in mugs. (Apple juice may be used instead of cider.)

Tom and Jerry (for 20)

1 bottle Bourbon or rye whiskey
½ bottle rum
12 eggs

6 tablespoons granulated sugar
1 teaspoon grated nutmeg
3 cups hot milk (or boiling water)

Beat the eggs until thick and light in color. Gradually add the sugar and nutmeg and continue beating until the batter is very thick. Chill for several hours. To serve, put 1 heaping tablespoon of the batter into each warm mug. Add ½ jigger rum and 1 jigger bourbon or rye. Fill the mug with hot milk (or boiling water) as desired. Stir and serve with a light grating of nutmeg on top. More liquor may be used but in the same proportion as above.

Wassail (30–40 cups)

12 eggs
4 bottles sherry or madeira
2 pounds sugar
1 teaspoon powdered nutmeg
2 teaspoons ginger
6 whole cloves
½ teaspoon mace
6 whole allspice
1 teaspoon ground cinnamon

In large pan mix the dry ingredients in ½ pint of water. Add the wine and let the mixture simmer over a very slow fire. Beat the egg yolks and whites separately and add these to the hot brew. Before serving, add several baked apples and lace the mixture well with brandy.

JULEPS

You will rarely find two people in any gathering who will agree as to what is or what is not a proper MINT JULEP. The recipe given is certainly an easy one to follow and is as good as they come.

Mint Julep
2 jiggers Bourbon
1 teaspoon powdered sugar
2 sprigs fresh mint
Club soda
Fill a Collins glass with crushed ice and set it aside. Strip the leaves from mint and muddle them in a small glass with the sugar. Add a small splash of soda, muddle again, and add the Bourbon. Stir and strain into the prepared glass over the ice. Work a long-handled spoon up and down in the mixture until the outside of the glass begins to frost. Decorate with sprigs of mint. Add more whiskey if desired. Sometimes the julep is topped with a splash of rum.
[Note: This same julep may be made with applejack, brandy, gin, rum, or rye whiskey. A CHAMPAGNE JULEP is also delicious but more champagne will be needed and perhaps a dash of brandy. The GIN MINT JULEP is frequently called a MAJOR BAILEY and may be served as a cocktail.]

LONG DRINKS

Americano
Place in a tumbler 2 jiggers
sweet vermouth and 1 jigger
Campari. Add 2 ice cubes and a
twist of lemon peel. Fill with
club soda.

American Punch
⅔ jigger brandy
⅔ jigger dry vermouth
1 teaspoon crème de menthe
Juice of ½ orange
½ teaspoon sugar
Shake juice, sugar, brandy, and
vermouth with cracked ice.
Strain into 10-ounce glass or
large goblet filled with shaved ice
and flavor with the crème de
menthe.

American Rose
1 jigger brandy
1 dash Pernod
1 teaspoon grenadine
2 slices of ripe peach, crushed
with a fork
Shake in a shaker with crushed
ice and strain into 10-ounce
glass. Fill with chilled champagne.

Angostura Highball
Place in a tumbler 2 ice cubes, 1
teaspoon Angostura bitters, and
fill with ginger ale.

Bermuda Highball
¾ jigger dry gin
¾ jigger brandy
½ jigger dry vermouth
Combine ingredients in highball
glass with ice cubes and fill with
ginger ale or club soda. Garnish
with lemon peel and serve.

Bishop
Fill a tumbler ½ full with
cracked ice. Add 1 teaspoon
sugar, juice of ½ lemon, and
juice of ½ orange. Fill with dry
red wine. Stir and add 1 slice of
orange and several dashes of
rum.

Black Rose
In a tumbler with 2 ice cubes place 1 teaspoon sugar and 1 jigger dark rum. Fill with cold black coffee. Stir and serve.

California Lemonade
1 jigger rye whiskey
1 dash grenadine
Juice of 1 lemon
Juice of 1 lime
1 tablespoon powdered sugar
Shake well with ice and strain into glass. Fill with chilled club soda.

Cassisco
Place 2 cubes of ice in a tumbler or large goblet. Add 1 tablespoon crème de cassis and 1 jigger brandy. Fill with club soda and serve.

Cincinnati
Fill a highball glass ½ full of beer. Fill up with chilled club soda and serve.

Cloak and Dagger
Fill a highball glass with ice cubes. Add 1½ jiggers Jamaica rum and fill with any cola drink. Add a generous twist of orange peel and a dash of orange bitters.

Cocoa Rickey
Place a scoop of vanilla ice cream in a large highball glass. Add 1 jigger crème de cacao and 1 tablespoon milk. Fill with club soda. Stir and add sugar if necessary.

Cuba Libre
Place 2 or 3 ice cubes in a large highball glass. Add 2 jiggers dark rum, the juice of ½ lime, and fill with any cola drink.

Doctor Funk
1⅔ jiggers dark rum
⅛ jigger Pernod
⅓ jigger lemon juice
⅛ jigger grenadine
¼ teaspoon sugar
1 lime
Cut lime in half and squeeze into shaker, dropping in the rinds also. Add all other ingredients and shake with crushed ice. Pour into 12-ounce glass and if necessary fill with club soda. Decorate with fruit if desired.

Dog's Nose
Place 1 or 2 jiggers gin in a tall highball glass. Fill up with cold beer or stout.

El Diablo
1 jigger tequila
⅓ jigger crème de cassis
½ lime
Ginger ale
Squeeze and drop the lime into highball glass. Add ice and other ingredients and fill with ginger ale.

Florida Special No. 2
2 jiggers dry gin
Juice of ½ orange
Rind of whole orange, cut in spiral form
Place orange rind in tall glass and add ice and other ingredi-

ents. Fill with ginger ale. (See Index.)

Fog Horn
Place 2 ice cubes in a highball glass. Add 2 jiggers dry gin and 1 slice of lemon. Fill with ginger beer and serve.

Frank's Refresher
Combine in a tumbler with 2 ice cubes, the juice of ½ lemon, 1 jigger raspberry syrup, and 1 jigger brandy. Fill with chilled champagne and serve.

Gin and Tonic
Place 2 jiggers dry gin in a high-ball glass with 2 or 3 ice cubes, and 1 slice of lemon. Fill with tonic water.

Gin Buck
Place the juice of ½ lime and 2 twists of lime peel in a highball glass with 2 jiggers dry gin and ice cubes. Fill up with ginger ale.

Golden Lemonade
1 jigger Danziger goldwasser
1 jigger Amer Picon
1 egg yolk
1 tablespoon powdered sugar
Juice of 2 limes
Shake well with cracked ice and strain into glass. Fill with chilled club soda.

Highball
Place in a 10-oz. glass ice cubes and 1 or 2 jiggers of any of the following: applejack, brandy, dry gin, rum, or any whiskey.

Fill glass with club soda or plain water and garnish, if desired, with a twist of lemon peel.

Lemonade (Plain)
Juice of ½ lemon
Juice of ½ lime
2 tablespoons powdered sugar
Shake well with ice and strain into tall glass. Add extra ice if desired and fill with chilled club soda. All lemon juice or all lime juice may be used instead of half and half. And to vary the drink, grenadine or other similar sweetening may be used instead of sugar. Sometimes an egg is shaken with the mixture.

Macka
Fill a tumbler ½ full with cracked ice. Add 1 dash crème de cassis and ⅓ each dry gin and sweet and dry vermouth. Stir well. Add slice of orange and serve.

Major Bailey
See "Juleps," note.

Mamie Taylor No. 2
In a large tumbler, with ice cubes, place 1 slice lemon and 2 jiggers dry gin or Scotch whisky. Fill with ginger ale. Stir and serve. (See Index.)

Modern Lemonade
1 jigger sherry
1 jigger sloe gin
2 tablespoons powdered sugar
Juice of 1 lemon
Stir well with ice and strain into

glass. Add twist of lemon peel and fill with chilled club soda.

Mojito

1⅓ jiggers Puerto Rican rum
½ lime
1 teaspoon sugar
Mint leaves

Squeeze lime into 10-ounce glass and drop in rind. Add other ingredients and fill ⅔ full with shaved ice. Add club soda, stir, and serve.

O'Hearn Special

2 jiggers brandy
1 twist orange peel
2 sprigs mint

Place in tall glass with ice cubes. Fill up with ginger ale. Stir and serve.

Pineapple Lemonade

1 jigger brandy
1 dash raspberry syrup
1 teaspoon powdered sugar
2 slices pineapple

Muddle the pineapple and sugar well in a shaker. Add other ingredients and shake well with ice. Strain into glass and decorate with twist of lemon peel and pineapple stick if desired.

Shandygaff

Fill tall glass half and half with chilled ale and ginger ale or ginger beer.

Spritzer

Place 2 jiggers white wine in highball glass with ice cubes and fill with club soda.

Stone Fence (Whisky)

2 jiggers Scotch whisky
½ teaspoon sugar
1 ice cube

Place in highball glass and fill with chilled club soda. Stir and serve. (See Index.)

Swedish Highball

2 jiggers Swedish punsch
1 dash bitters

Place in highball glass with ice cubes and fill up with chilled club soda.

Tomate

Place in highball glass ice cubes, 2 dashes Pernod, and 1 teaspoon grenadine. Fill with plain water as desired.

PUFFS

All "puffs" contain milk and are served in small tumblers.

Brandy Puff

Place 1 or 2 ice cubes in a glass and add 1 or 2 jiggers brandy and 1 or 2 jiggers milk. Fill with chilled club soda or tonic water, stir gently, and serve.

The GIN, RUM, or WHISKEY PUFF is made the same as above, substituting the desired liquor.

PUNCHES AND EGGNOGS

Applejack Punch (25–30 cups)
2 bottles applejack
4 jiggers grenadine
1 pint orange juice
Combine the ingredients in a punch bowl with a block of ice. Just before serving add 2 quarts chilled ginger ale. Decorate with fruit if desired.

Artillery Punch (25–30 cups)
1 quart strong tea
1 bottle rye whiskey
1 bottle red wine
1 pint Jamaica rum
½ pint dry gin
½ pint brandy
1 jigger Bénédictine
1 pint orange juice
½ pint lemon juice
Combine all ingredients in a large punch bowl with a block of ice. If too dry, sugar syrup may be added. Decorate with twists of lemon peel.

Bacardi Punch
Fill a tall glass with shaved ice. Pour in ½ jigger grenadine and 2 jiggers Bacardi rum. Stir until glass is frosted and decorate with fruit.

Baccio (for 8)
Combine in a large punch bowl with a block of ice 5 jiggers grapefruit juice, 5 jiggers dry gin, 2 jiggers anisette, and slices of orange and lemon. Add a little sugar syrup to taste. Just before serving pour in 1 split chilled club soda and 1 split chilled champagne. Stir slightly.

Baltimore Eggnog (for 10)
Separate the whites and yolks of 12 eggs. Beat with the egg yolks 1 pound powdered sugar. Stir in slowly 1 pint brandy, ½ pint light rum, ½ pint peach brandy, 3

pints milk, and 1 pint heavy
cream. Chill thoroughly and fold
in stiffly beaten egg whites before
serving.

Basic Eggnog
Combine in a shaker with ice 2
jiggers brandy or light rum, 1
egg, 1 tablespoon sugar, and ¾
cup milk. Shake well and strain
into glass. Sprinkle with nutmeg.

Best Punch (10–12 cups)
1 cup strong tea
Juice of 2 lemons
1 teaspoon sugar
2 jiggers brandy
1 jigger curaçao
1 jigger New England rum
Place a large block of ice in a
punch bowl. Add the above ingredients. Just before serving,
add 1 quart chilled club soda
and 1 quart chilled champagne.

Bombay Punch (2 gallons)
Combine in a mixing bowl, without ice, 1 quart brandy, 1 quart
sherry, ¼ pint maraschino, ½ orange curaçao, and 2 quarts
chilled club soda. Set punch
bowl in a bed of crushed ice,
decorate with fruits as desired,
and just before serving add 4
quarts chilled champagne.

Bourbon Eggnog (for 12)
Beat yolks and whites of 8 eggs
separately, adding ½ pound
sugar to the whites. Combine
beaten yolks and whites and
blend gently. Stir in 2 jiggers rum
and 1 bottle Bourbon whiskey,

1 pint heavy cream, and 1 quart
milk. Mix all together and chill
thoroughly. Serve with grated
nutmeg on top.

Bowle (for 15–20)
[Strawberry (Erdbeer Bowle)–1
pint strawberries, washed and
hulled; peach (Pfirsich Bowle)–
4 ripe peaches, peeled and
halved; pineapple (Ananas
Bowle)–2 cups diced fresh pineapple; orange (Apfelsinen
Bowle)–3 oranges, peeled and
sectioned, plus grated rind of
one; or raspberry (Himbeer
Bowle)–1 pint raspberries,
washed and picked over.] Put
fruit in punch bowl with ¼ cup
sugar. Place bowl in refrigerator
for a couple of hours. When
ready to serve, pour in 3 bottles
chilled Moselle or Rhine wine
and 1 bottle any sparkling wine
or 1 quart club soda.

Brandy Eggnog
Prepare same as BOURBON EGG-
NOG, using brandy instead of
Bourbon.

Brandy Punch (25–30 cups)
Juice of 15 lemons
Juice of 4 oranges
1¼ pounds powdered sugar
½ pint curaçao
1 or 2 jiggers grenadine
2 quarts brandy
Place in punch bowl with large
block of ice and just before serving add 1 or 2 quarts club soda.

Breakfast Eggnog

1 fresh egg
¾ jigger brandy
¼ jigger curaçao
¼ glass milk

Shake well with ice and strain into tall glass. Grate nutmeg on top.

Bride's Bowl (for 20)

Dice 2 cups fresh pineapple and place in a punch bowl with ½ cup sugar syrup, 1 cup lemon juice, 1½ cups unsweetened pineapple juice, 1⅓ cups peach brandy, and 1½ or 2 bottles medium rum. Add block of ice and before serving pour in 2 quarts chilled club soda and 1 pint sliced strawberries.

Buddha Punch (for 10)

½ bottle Rhine wine
4 jiggers orange juice
4 jiggers lemon juice
2 jiggers curaçao
2 jiggers medium rum
1 dash Angostura bitters

Combine in punch bowl with block of ice and just before serving add 1 quart chilled club soda and 1 bottle chilled champagne. Garnish with twists of lemon peel and mint leaves.

Burgundy Punch (for 15)

Combine in a punch bowl with a block of ice 2 bottles red burgundy, 5 jiggers port, 3 jiggers cherry brandy, juice of 3 lemons, juice of 6 oranges, 1 or 2 tablespoons sugar, and a long twist each lemon and orange peel. Just before serving add 2 bottles chilled club soda.

Calypso Punch (for 4–8)

3 cups CocoRibe
2 cups orange juice
2 cups cold water
⅔ cup lemon juice
⅓ cup grenadine
1 pint lemon or orange sherbet

Combine all ingredients in a punch bowl with block of ice. Float sherbet in scoop measures.

Cardinal Punch (for 25–30)

Place 1½ pounds sugar in a punch bowl and dissolve with 2 quarts club soda. Add 2 bottles red bordeaux, 1 pint brandy, 1 pint rum, 1 jigger sweet vermouth, 1 sliced orange, and 2 or 3 slices fresh pineapple. Stir and add block of ice. Just before serving add 1 pint of any sparkling white wine.

Christmas Punch No. 2 (50 cups)

In a large punch bowl combine 1 quart strong tea with a bottle each rum, rye whiskey, and brandy, ½ bottle Bénédictine, 1 tablespoon Angostura bitters, and 1 sliced pineapple. Add the juice of 12 oranges, ½ or 1 pound sugar, dissolved in water, and mix together thoroughly. Add block of ice and just before serving pour in 2 bottles chilled champagne.

Claret Punch No. 1
Fill a tall glass ½ full of cracked ice. Add 1 teaspoon each lemon juice, grenadine, and curaçao. Fill with red bordeaux or burgundy and decorate with slice of orange. Serve with a straw.

Claret Punch No. 2 (for 10–15)
Mix together 2 bottles red bordeaux, ¼ pound sugar, and the rind of 1 lemon. Chill for several hours. Place block of ice in a punch bowl and pour in the chilled mixture. Add 1½ jiggers cognac, 1½ jiggers curaçao, and 1½ jiggers dry sherry. Before serving pour in 2 pints chilled club soda.

CocoRibe Eggnog (for 6)
6 eggs, separated
¼ cup plus 2 tablespoons sugar
2 cups heavy cream
2 cups CocoRibe
1 dash nutmeg
Beat egg whites until foamy. Beat in ¼ cup sugar. Beat yolks with remaining sugar. Fold yolks into whites. Add cream, milk, and CocoRibe. Stir well and chill. Pour into punch bowl and sprinkle with nutmeg.

Colonial Tea Punch (12–15 cups)
Remove the peel in thin strips from 12 lemons and place the strips in a punch bowl. Add 1 quart strong tea and the juice from the lemons. Mix with 2 cups sugar and let stand for 1 hour. Add 1 quart dark rum and

1 jigger brandy. Pour the mixture over crushed ice and serve.

Curaçao Punch
Place in a large glass ½ teaspoon sugar, the juice of ½ lemon, 1 jigger curaçao, and 1 jigger brandy or rum. Fill with shaved ice and stir lightly. Decorate with fruit if desired and serve with a straw.

Dragoon Punch
See Index, CHAMPAGNE PUNCH NO. 7.

Dubonnet Party Punch (15–20 glasses)
Pour 1 bottle Dubonnet into a large pitcher and add 1 pint dry gin, the juice and rind of 6 limes, and 1 quart of chilled club soda. Fill tall glasses with crushed ice and decorate with mint. Pour in the punch.

Fish House Punch No. 1 (for 25–30)
Dissolve ¾ pound sugar in a large punch bowl with a little water. When entirely dissolved, stir in 1 quart lemon juice, 2 bottles Jamaica rum, 2 quarts water, and peach brandy to taste. Place large block of ice in punch bowl and allow mixture to chill 2 hours. Serve in punch glasses.

Fish House Punch No. 2 (for 40)
Dissolve in a punch bowl 1½ cups sugar in 1 cup water and 3 cups lemon juice. Add 3 pints dry white wine, 1 bottle dark

rum, 1 bottle golden rum, 1 bottle brandy, and 2½ jiggers peach brandy. Let the mixture stand for 2 or 3 hours, stirring it occasionally. Before serving add a block of ice, stir to cool and serve. If a stronger punch is desired, do not add the block of ice to the punch bowl but set the bowl in a bed of crushed ice to chill.

Gin Punch No. 1
Place in a tall glass 1 lump sugar, 1 twist lemon peel, juice of ½ lemon, 2 dashes maraschino, and 2 jiggers dry gin. Add cracked ice and fill with club soda. Stir and serve.

Gin Punch No. 2 (for 12)
Combine the juice of 12 lemons, the juice of 20 oranges, 2 bottles dry gin, and 4 jiggers grenadine. Pour over large block of ice. Add 2 bottles chilled club soda. Decorate with fruit as desired and serve.

Happy South (for 20–25)
1 bottle Southern Comfort
1 cup pineapple juice
½ cup lemon juice
2 bottles champagne, or other sparkling wine
Mix in punch bowl, with block of ice, adding the sparkling ingredient at the last minute.

Heavenly Vin Blanc (for 35)
3 bottles dry white wine
¼ bottle brandy
6 oz. Bénédictine
½ pound pineapple, chopped

½ bottle sparkling water, chilled
Marinate pineapple in brandy. Mix everything except sparkling water in large punch bowl. Put in refrigerator for 1 to 2 hours. Add sparkling water just before serving.

Huckle-My-Butt (for 6)
1 quart cold beer or ale
1 pint cold brandy
2 whole eggs, beaten
Sugar to taste
1 pinch each cinnamon, cloves, nutmeg
Serve in tumblers or small mugs.

Instant Eggnog (for 10)
Place 2 quarts French vanilla ice cream in a punch bowl. Add 1 bottle Bourbon whiskey and 3 jiggers Jamaica rum. Stir until creamy and sprinkle with nutmeg. Serve in punch cups.

Ladies' Punch
Combine in a shaker 2 tablespoons powdered sugar, 1 egg, ½ jigger maraschino, 1 jigger crème de cacao, 1 twist orange peel, 1 cup milk, and 2 dashes nutmeg. Shake well with ice and strain into glass. Serve with additional nutmeg on top.

Milk Punch (Basic)
[Note: The following recipe may be used for applejack, brandy, rum, or whiskey.]
Combine in a shaker with cracked ice 1 or 2 jiggers any liquor desired, 1 cup milk, and 1 tablespoon powdered sugar. Shake well and strain into glass. Sprinkle with nutmeg.

"Misch" House Punch (for 20)
½ bottle dry gin
½ bottle Campari
1 quart orange juice
Stir together in a large bowl with ice cubes. Remove ice cubes and when ready to serve add 1 bottle cold champagne or other sparkling white wine.

Myrtle Bank Punch
Combine in shaker with a large piece of ice 1 jigger dark rum (151 proof), juice of ½ lime, 6 dashes grenadine, and 1 teaspoon sugar. Shake and pour over cracked ice in a 10-ounce glass. Float maraschino on top.

Navy Punch (for 10)
Slice 4 pineapples and sprinkle well with 1 pound fine sugar. Add ½ bottle dark rum, ½ bottle cognac, ½ bottle peach brandy, and the juice of 4 lemons. Chill well. Pour into punch bowl with block of ice. Decorate with fruit as desired and add 4 quarts of chilled champagne or sparkling wine.

Nourmahal Punch
Squeeze ½ lime and drop it into a 10-ounce glass with cracked ice. Add 2 jiggers rum, 2 dashes Angostura bitters and fill with club soda.

Nuremberg (for 15)
Place ¾ pound sugar in a large bowl and strain over it through a fine sieve the juice of 2 or 3 large oranges. Add twists of the peel cut very thin and pour in 1 quart boiling water, ⅓ quart arrack, 1 bottle of red wine. Stir all together. Pour into tall glasses over cracked ice.

Open Condominium (for 25)
1 bottle Southern Comfort
6 oz. lemon juice
3 quarts 7-Up
1 6-oz. can frozen lemonade
1 6-oz. can frozen orange juice
Mix in punch bowl. Decorate with fruit slices. Add a chunk of ice when ready to serve.

Patrick Gavin Duffy's Punch
Combine in a shaker with ice 2 jiggers brandy, 1 jigger Bénédictine, ½ teaspoon powdered sugar and juice of 1 orange. Shake well and pour into tall glass. Decorate with mint and fruit if desired. Serve with a straw.

Peach Melba Punch (for 30)
Dip 6–8 peaches in boiling water so that the skins slip off. Puncture the peaches with the tines of a fork. Put in punch bowl with 1 pint brandy. Add 1 cup crème de cassis. Put a block of ice in punch bowl. Add 4 chilled bottles of sparkling wine when ready to serve.

Pendennis Eggnog (for 8–10)
Mix together 1 pound powdered sugar and 1 bottle Bourbon whiskey. Let stand for 2 hours. Separate 12 eggs and beat the yolks to a froth, adding the

sweetened whiskey slowly. Let this stand for 2 hours. Whip 2 quarts heavy cream until stiff and whip the egg whites. Fold these separately into the whiskey mixture and chill. This is one of the richest of all eggnogs.

Pineapple Punch (for 10)
1½ quarts Moselle
Juice of 3 lemons
5 dashes Angostura bitters
2½ jiggers dry gin
⅔ jigger pine syrup
⅔ jigger grenadine
⅔ jigger maraschino
Pour all together into punch bowl with 1 quart chilled club soda. Set bowl in bed of crushed ice to chill. Decorate with pineapple.

Pisco Punch
In a large wineglass or small tumbler place 1 ice cube with a teaspoon each of pineapple and lemon juice. Add 2 jiggers brandy and a small wedge of pineapple. Fill with cold water. Stir well and serve.

Plantation Punch
Combine in a large old-fashioned glass 1 jigger Southern Comfort, ½ jigger lemon juice, ½ jigger rum, and 1 teaspoon sugar. Fill with ice and a little club soda. Garnish with a twist of orange peel and serve.

Porch Party Punch (for 8–10)
3 cups cranberry-apple drink
1 quart club soda

2 cups CocoRibe
½ cup Triple Sec or Cointreau
¼ cup lime juice
Stir ingredients in a large pitcher with fruit slices and ice.

Quintet (for 30–40)
3 jiggers brandy
3 jiggers dark rum
4 bottles dry white wine
Juice of 8 lemons
Juice of 8 oranges
Combine in punch bowl and let stand an hour. Add block of ice and fruit garnish. Just before serving pour in 2 bottles chilled club soda.

Regent Punch (for 10–12)
2½ jiggers brandy
2½ jiggers Swedish punsch
1¼ jiggers curaçao
1 pint Jamaica rum
Juice of 6 lemons
1 cup strong tea
1 teaspoon Angostura bitters
1½ quarts champagne
Combine all the ingredients except the champagne in a punch bowl set in a bed of crushed ice. Just before serving, pour in the champagne and garnish with fruit as desired.

Rhine Wine Punch (for 10–12)
2 quarts Rhine wine
1 pint chilled club soda
2 jiggers brandy
2 jiggers maraschino
½ cup strong tea
⅓ pound powdered sugar
Combine all the ingredients in a

punch bowl set in a bed of crushed ice. Decorate with fruit as desired and serve when thoroughly chilled.

Roman Punch (for 10)

2½ jiggers brandy
2½ jiggers Swedish punsch
1¼ jiggers curaçao
1 pint Jamaica rum
Juice of 6 lemons
1½ quarts chilled champagne
1 teaspoon Angostura or orange bitters
1 cup strong tea

Combine all the ingredients in a punch bowl set in a bed of crushed ice. Garnish with fruit as desired and serve when thoroughly chilled. (Framboise may be used instead of the curaçao.)

Rum Cow

1 jigger Puerto Rican rum
2 drops vanilla
1 pinch nutmeg
1 dash Angostura bitters
1 cup milk
2 teaspoons sugar

Shake well with ice and pour into a tall glass. (This is a specific for the morning after.)

Rum Eggnog

Prepare same as BOURBON EGGNOG, using Jamaica rum instead of Bourbon whiskey.

Rum Punch (for 100)

10 bottles white wine
2 pounds brown sugar
2 quarts orange juice
1 quart lemon juice
10 sliced bananas
2 fresh pineapples, cut up or chopped

Place the fruit juice, orange and lemon rinds, bananas, pineapple, and wine in a crock with the sugar. Cover and let stand overnight. In the morning add 5 bottles light rum, 1 bottle Jamaica rum, and 1 bottle crème de banane. Let stand until just before the party. Strain into punch bowl with ice as needed. Taste for seasoning and add either sugar syrup or lemon juice as desired.

Rye Whiskey Punch

Shake with plenty of chopped ice 1 teaspoon lemon juice, 2 teaspoons sugar, and 2 jiggers rye whiskey. Pour unstrained into 10-ounce glass and decorate with slice of orange.

Sauterne Punch No. 1

Fill a 10-ounce glass ½ full of cracked ice. Add ½ teaspoon sugar, juice of ½ lemon, and 1 or 2 teaspoons curaçao. Fill with sauterne. Stir and decorate with fruit as desired. Serve with a straw.

Sauterne Punch No. 2 (for 10)

½ pound powdered sugar
2 bottles sauterne
2½ jiggers maraschino
2½ jiggers curaçao
2½ jiggers Grand Marnier

Combine ingredients in a punch bowl with a large block of ice.

Add several long twists of lemon and orange peel and mint if desired. Serve when well chilled.

Savannah Punch (for 15)
1 quart brandy
1 quart dark rum
1 pint pineapple juice
1 pint lemon juice
1 pint orange juice
½ cup sugar
Mix well over a chunk of ice.

Scotch Whisky Punch (for 10–12)
Combine in a pitcher with cracked ice 1 quart Scotch whisky, juice and rind of 3 lemons, ½ cup sugar, and 1 quart club soda. Stir and pour into goblets with extra ice and garnish with fruit as desired.

Strawberry Punch
Place ½ teaspoon sugar in a 10-ounce glass. Add a little water to dissolve and the juice of ½ lemon and 1 or 2 teaspoons strawberry syrup. Fill ⅔ with shaved ice and pour in 2 jiggers brandy. Stir and decorate with strawberries. Serve with a spoon and straw.

Whiskey Punch (for 25–30)
Place a block of ice in a punch bowl and pour over it the juice of 6 lemons, the juice of 8 oranges, 2 tablespoons sugar, and 2 jiggers curaçao. Stir and pour in 2 quarts of rye, Bourbon, or blended whiskey. Add fruits as desired and 2 quarts chilled club soda. Stir and serve. (1 quart of iced tea may be substituted for 1 quart of club soda.)

Xalapa Punch (for 20–25)
Place the grated peel of 2 lemons in a punch bowl and pour over it 2½ quarts strong hot tea. Let this stand for 10 or 15 minutes and add 1 pint sugar syrup. Let cool. When cold add 1 quart applejack, 1 quart light rum, and 1 bottle dry red wine. Just before serving add a block of ice and 1 lemon, sliced thin. Serve when well chilled.

Young People's Punch (for 25)
Combine in a punch bowl ½ pint sugar syrup, ½ pint lemon juice, 1 pint orange juice, 2½ jiggers curaçao, 2½ jiggers pineapple juice, 1½ jiggers maraschino, and 2 bottles red wine. Chill with a block of ice and just before serving add 2 quarts of club soda. This punch is excellent when spiked with brandy as your judgment dictates.

RICKEYS

[Note: A rickey is always made of squeezed citrus juice, liquor of your choice, and club soda. Most rickeys are made with the following recipe, using 1 or 2 jiggers of applejack, gin, rum, or whiskey.]

Basic Rickey
Place 1 cube of ice in a medium tumbler with ½ lime or ¼ lemon lightly squeezed. Pour in liquor desired and fill with chilled club soda. Serve with lime or lemon rind in the glass.

Hugo Rickey
Make the same as BASIC RICKEY, adding 2 dashes grenadine and 1 slice pineapple.

Puerto Rico Rickey
Make the same as BASIC RICKEY, adding 2 dashes raspberry syrup.

SANGAREES

[Note: A sangaree is always served in a tumbler which may be either small or large, depending on the ingredients used. Regardless of size, it will always have a grating of nutmeg a-top.]

Ale, Porter, or Stout Sangaree
Place in a large tumbler ½ teaspoon sugar dissolved in a little water. Fill with chilled ale, porter, or stout. Stir very slightly and serve with a sprinkling of nutmeg.

Brandy Sangaree
Place in a small tumbler ½ teaspoon sugar dissolved in a little water. Add 1 jigger brandy and ice. Stir and serve with a sprinkling of nutmeg. (Gin, port, rum, sherry, or whiskey may be used instead of brandy.)

SANGRIA

This immensely popular drink may be made from any cut-up fruit and a reasonably dry red wine (some people are now using dry white). Peaches are the usual fruit. Originally, Spanish Rioja was the wine. The standard recipe, for 4, is as follows: Combine in a pitcher 1 bottle red or white wine, juice of 2 oranges, juice of 1 lemon, ¼ cup sugar, and 2 jiggers brandy or Grand Marnier. Add a few fruit rinds. Chill well or add ice.

SCAFFAS

[Note: Scaffas are drinks served unchilled, undiluted, in cocktail glasses.]

Brandy Scaffa
Place in a cocktail glass 1 dash Angostura bitters and 1½ jiggers each maraschino and brandy. Stir and serve.

Gin Scaffa
Place in a cocktail glass 1 dash Angostura bitters and 1½ jiggers each Bénédictine and dry gin. Stir and serve.

Rum Scaffa
Place in a cocktail glass 1 dash Angostura bitters and 1½ jiggers each Bénédictine and rum. Stir and serve.

Whiskey Scaffa
Place in a cocktail glass 1 dash Angostura bitters and 1½ jiggers each Bénédictine and whiskey. Stir and serve.

SHRUBS

[Note: Shrubs are drinks that may be served either hot or cold but almost always from a large pitcher. And when cold, served with plenty of ice and a fruit garnish.]

Brandy Shrub
To the thin peel of 2 firm lemons and the juice of 5, add 2 quarts of brandy. Cover and let stand for 3 days, then add 1 quart sweet sherry and 2 pounds granulated sugar. Stir well and strain through a fine sieve. Bottle and cork tightly.

Currant Shrub

Boil gently for 10 minutes 2 cups granulated sugar with 1 pint of strained currant juice, skimming frequently. Let cool and when lukewarm add ¾ cup brandy. Bottle and cork tightly.

Rum Shrub

Combine in a crock 1 pint orange juice, ¼ pound granulated sugar, and 1 quart rum. Cover well and let stand. Then strain, bottle, and cork tightly.

SLINGS

Brandy Sling

Place in a highball glass 3 cubes of ice, 1 dash Angostura bitters, the juice of ½ lemon, 1 teaspoon sugar, and 2 jiggers brandy. Fill with plain water, stir well, and serve.

Gin Sling

Place 1 teaspoon powdered sugar in a highball glass with 2 jiggers dry gin and several cubes of ice. Fill with plain water, stir well, and serve. (Club soda may be used instead of plain water.)

Singapore Gin Sling

Combine in a shaker 1⅓ jiggers dry gin, ⅔ jigger cherry brandy, 1 teaspoon sugar, juice of ½ lemon, and 1 dash Angostura bitters. Shake well with ice and strain into a tall glass. Add ice and club soda as desired. Twist lemon peel over top and garnish with fruit or mint. A dash of Bénédictine may be added.

Straits Sling (for 6)

8 jiggers dry gin
2 jiggers Bénédictine
2 jiggers cherry brandy
Juice of 2 lemons
1 teaspoon Angostura bitters
1 teaspoon orange bitters
Shake well with ice and strain into glasses. Fill with chilled club soda as desired and garnish with fruit.

Vodka Sling

Prepare same as GIN SLING, using vodka instead of gin.

SMASHES

[Note: Smashes are nothing more than junior-size juleps. They are served in small tumblers or old-fashioned glasses. Brandy, gin, rum, or any whiskey may be used for this.]

Basic Smash
Place 1 scant teaspoon powdered sugar in a glass with 2 sprigs fresh mint and a few drops of water. Crush the mint with a muddler and fill glass half full of shaved ice. Pour in 1 or 2 jiggers of liquor and, if desired, a squirt of club soda. Decorate with mint and serve.

TODDIES

[Note: Toddies, when served cold, are all made the same way, whether applejack, brandy, gin, rum, or whiskey is used. For hot toddies, see "Hot Drinks."]

Basic Toddy
Place in a small tumbler or old-fashioned glass 1 scant teaspoon sugar. Dissolve with a little water. Add 1 or 2 cubes of ice and 2 jiggers of the desired liquor. Stir and serve.

ZOOMS

[Note: A zoom is a drink combining spirits, honey, and cream.]

Rum Zoom
Dissolve in a cup 1 teaspoon honey in a little boiling water. Pour into a shaker with 1 teaspoon cream and 2 jiggers rum. Add ice and shake well and strain into glass. (Brandy, gin, or whiskey may be used instead of rum.)

WINE

Vino: vidit, vicit (wine: it saw, it conquered). I doubt if any Roman ever spake these words, but they will serve to suggest that wine, while perhaps not "conquering" as yet, definitely came and saw. A decade ago, we in the United States drank less than a gallon a year per person. Today, the figure is two gallons plus. The optimists claim five gallons by 1985. While perhaps not a boom, that's certainly a boomlet, but we have a long way to go.

Hear this: France drinks twenty-nine gallons per person per year; Italy and Portugal, twenty-eight gallons; Argentina, twenty-two. But we are not a Latin country, where food and wine are synonymous. Even Germany, with all its Rhine wines, drinks less than eight gallons per person, per year. The U.S.S.R., while no world-beater with 3.9 gallons, beats us!

Compare: vis-à-vis that anemic two gallons, we consume twenty-six gallons of coffee, twenty-seven gallons of milk, twenty-five gallons of beer, and (surprise, surprise) thirteen gallons of tea. Fruit juices that you hear so much about only ring up four gallons. Incidentally, today our top wine-drinking areas—California and the District of Columbia—are already drinking that optimum five gallons.

WHAT WINES DO WE DRINK?

About 82 percent of the wine we drink is (the U.S. wine makers hate the word) "domestic"; the rest imported. Of the 82 percent, 85 percent is from California and its neighboring states of Oregon,

Washington, and Idaho; 10 to 12 percent is from New York; and the small remainder is from all the other states.

On the foreign scene, would you believe that today over 60 percent of all our imports speak Italian? Here's the line-up for the first five imports by brand in 1982: Riunite, 11 million cases; Cella, 2,750,000; Folonari, 1,735,000; Bolla, 1,620,000; Zonin, 1,300,000—all Italian. The next five, in order, are Giacobazzi (Italy), Blue Nun (Germany), Mateus (Portugal), Canei (Italy), and Yago (Spain). French wines, in terms of quantity (not quality), is way down there near the bottom.

WHAT TYPE OF WINE DO WE DRINK?

All wine is basically the juice of the grape into which yeast is insinuated. The yeast attacks the sugar in the must (juice) and converts it to alcohol. Presto, changeo! No more grape juice!—Wine!

There are four kinds of wine:

1. *Table wine.* This is wine drunk at table, with food; its alcoholic strength ranges from 9.5 to 14 percent. This is by far the largest category—about 80 percent—of wine drunk in the United States. It was not always so—seventy years ago it represented only 20 percent, with almost 80 percent being dessert wine, the next category.

2. *Dessert, or fortified, wine.* This is wine which has been "fortified," for the most part by the addition of brandy, to produce a strength of 17 to 21 percent alcohol. Sherry, madeira, and port are popular dessert wines.

3. *Sparkling wine.* This is wine that is effervescent because of CO_2 gas produced by fermentation a second time—in the bottle (*méthode champenoise,* or "transfer") or in a pressurized tank (the Charmat, or bulk method). Even simple carbonation may be used, but not often. It will tell you on the label.

4. *Flavored, or apéritif, wine.* This is simply normal wine into which berries, barks, roots, or flowers have been steeped. Vermouth is the best known. Some are proprietary, made according to secret formulas.

COLOR

Another wine differentiation can be made according to color: red, white, or pink. Today, white table wines represent nearly 60 percent of the wine Americans drink; red, about 25 percent; and pink (rosé), the other 15 percent. In 1960 the color chart looked like this: white, 17 percent; red, 74 percent; and pink, 9 percent. What a flipflop we've made to whites and even pinks—both served cold! There's your reason—*cold*. America likes drinks cold. (That's why I've become an advocate of cooling the lesser red wines, too. Doesn't hurt them a bit. Matter of fact, a little chilling can cover a multitude of sins.)

THE WINES OF THE WORLD

UNITED STATES

There are two major categories of American wine: (1) California and other West Coast wines. (2) New York and other East Coast wines.

West Coast

1. Varietals: The top wines, named for the variety of the grapes that make them (by law now, 75 percent must be of the name variety; it used to be 51 percent).

Red—cabernet sauvignon, zinfandel, pinot noir.

White—chardonnay, sauvignon blanc, Johannisberg riesling, chenin blanc, French colombard.

2. Generics: Wines that parrot the European wine regions and aim to suggest their wines, such as chablis, burgundy, champagne, bordeaux, sauterne, etc.

3. Monopole or proprietaries: One maker's trade-mark or specialty wine, e.g., *Masson's* Emerald Dry, *Gallo's* Hearty Burgundy, etc.

East Coast

1. Labruscas: Wines made from native American grapes that were growing here before Columbus discovered the place—concord, scuppernong, catawba, niagara, etc. Some can be quite decent. Most are grapey (winemen use the word "foxy"). Popular brands are Taylor, Gold Seal, Great Western, and Widmer.

2. Viniferas: Wines made from European transplants, the same as they are in California—chardonnay, riesling, etc. These grapes are not truly hardy in Eastern winters, so that the fortunes of the wine industry are in the lap of Mother Nature, who isn't always kind. Konstantin Frank, Gold Seal, Glenora, and other New York state Finger Lakes producers do a fine, though limited, job.

3. Hybrids: I choose to think the eastern wine future lies in the

French-American hybrid grapes, such as seyval blanc, vidal blanc, Marshal Foch, chelois, and baco noir. These combine the hardihood of the native American grapes and the wine-making qualities of the French. Many makers—order by grape name.

4. Sparklers: New York State is one of the largest producers of sparkling wines in the nation, if not the largest. Popular brands are Taylor, Great Western, Widmer's, and Gold Seal.

FRANCE

France is fond of the old adage: "Fifty percent of the great wines of the world come from France; 50 percent of the great wines of France come from Bordeaux." That may be a bit overweening, but it's not too far from the truth. French wines from Bordeaux, Burgundy, and Champagne and the somewhat lesser ones from the Loire and Rhone valleys, Alsace, the Midi, and Provence represent the cream of the crop.

Bordeaux

Five hundred million bottles a year! That's how much is produced in France's largest wine-growing region—an area centering on the Atlantic port city of Bordeaux and comprising the land around the confluence of the Dordogne, Garonne, and Gironde rivers. The region is particularly noted for the famous châteaux wines—Lafite, Margaux, Latour, Mouton-Rothschild, Haut-Brion, Ausone, Cheval-Blanc, Pétrus, d'Yquem. These are the top, top wines of Bordeaux—nay, of the world. There are hundreds of others, some few "classified" in 1855, but most not.

The nomenclature, of that classification, A.O.C., or *"Appéllation Controllé,"* appears on France's best bottles and will help you find the top. What happened was that in 1855, a World's Fair was to be held in Paris and its organizers asked Bordeaux for its "best wines." But which were "best"? By means of tasting panels and recourse to records of prices paid, the Bordelaise selected some sixty-five from the Médoc, Graves, and Sauterne districts as top wines. Wines from St. Émilion have been added since, but even today, Pomerol wines are not codified.

Burgundy

Burgundy, France's second greatest wine-growing region, is in east-central France. It comprises separated districts in what was once the province of Burgundy. The largest of these is the Côte d'Or;

smaller ones are Chablis and Beaujolais. The Burgundy region produces only about one third as much wine as Bordeaux.

The three main kinds of wine from Burgundy are:

1. The run-of-the-mill table wines with proprietary names and little-known antecedents.

2. The village wines such as Aloxe-Corton and Gevrey-Chambertin, which combine the village names (Aloxe, Gevrey) with the names of the top vineyard of the area (Corton, Chambertin). Any decent wines of a village can use such names even though they don't contain a drop of wine from the area's top vineyard.

3. The top-drawer wines from one estate or vineyard. Among the reds are Chambertin, Corton, Clos de Vougeot, Musigny, Richebourg, Bonnes Mares, Nuits St. Georges, Grands Echézaux, and Romanée-Conti. Among the whites are Corton-Charlemagne, Meursault, Montrachet, Bâtard-Montrachet, Chevalier-Montrachet, Puligny-Montrachet, and some of the Grand Crus and Premier Crus Chablis.

Many Burgundy connoisseurs consider the red wines of the Domaine de la Romanée-Conti as the greatest in the world. And many consider Montrachet and its family of hyphenations—Bâtard, Chevalier, Puligny—as the greatest whites.

Chablis, north of the Côte d'Or, produces its own hierarchy of great whites—but in small quantities, mind you. There would seem to be little excuse for using the word "chablis" to represent some undistinguished white blends the world over.

Macon, south of the Côte d'Or, produces similar white wines made from the same grape (chardonnay), lots less costly. The wines of Macon may call themselves burgundies.

Beaujolais, just south of Macon, produces wines entitled to the use of the term burgundy but its red wines are very different—made from the gamay grape instead of the only grape legal for true red Burgundy—the pinot noir. That doesn't reduce the great popularity of Beaujolais one whit.

Most vineyards and properties in the Burgundy region are multi-owned—by fathers, sons, daughters, neighbors—and their cousins and their aunts. That's why, in Burgundy, the wine shipper and/or negotiant's name is vitally important. Get to know a few of the names you can bank on—Chanson, Louis Latour, Bouchard, Robert Drouhin, Chauvenet, Faively, Jaboulet-Vercherre, Jadot, Labouré-Roi, Prosper Maufoux, Leroy, Mommessin, Patriarche, Piat, Thorin, Rodet, Geisweiler, Duboeuf, D'Angerville, Bize, Pic, Dujac, Moillard, Point, Prieur, Ropiteau, Rousseau, Henri Gouges, Dujac, Hubert de Montille, Domaine de la Pousse d'Or, and a host of others.

Rhone

This huge wine area along the banks of the great river Rhone—one hundred and forty miles long, from Vienne to Avignon—gives us both good and fair wines, white and red and pink.

The reds include Hermitage, Gigondas, Côte Rotie, and the vastly popular Chateauneuf-du-Pape.

Among the whites are Hermitage, Condrieu, and Château Grillet. (I include Grillet as a matter of interest only. Don't look too hard— the whole vineyard is three acres, and the production is 1,700 U.S. gallons a year. It is the smallest A.O.C. district of France. Charlemagne was once the owner!)

And, oh! yes, the pinks. Don't let me pass over Tavel, the first, and still probably the best, rosé of the world.

Loire

This is wine area along the banks of another river, in west-central France, the lovely Loire, where the kings of France reared their pleasure domes. Vouvray is its most varied wine—dry, sweet, or semi-sweet, still or sparkling—and sometimes quite good. Bourgueil and Chinon are pleasant reds. Pouilly Fumé and Sancerre are the twin blessings of the Loire, along with Muscadet, made in Brittany, at the mouth of the Loire. It is Brittany's only A.O.C. wine and a wonderful accompaniment to her fish and shellfish—and to yours.

Alsace

This is the French equivalent of the Rhineland, an extension of the vineyards of the Rhine and Mosel, at the northeastern edge of France. All the Alsatian wines are varietals and 100 percent of the grapes from which they take their names.

Riesling is the preeminent wine of Alsace, as it is of Germany, but gewürztraminer has lately made a huge niche for itself. *Gewürz* means spicy and the gewürztraminer grape is a superior clone of the older traminer grape. Sylvaner wine is the third, made from the work horse sylvaner grape, and generally a peg below the other two. Zwicker and Edelzwicker are the Alsatian words for blends.

Champagne

The queen. In France (and recently in Japan, Great Britain, Spain, Canada, and some other countries), no wine may be called "Champagne" or sold as such, unless it is made in a clearly demarcated area of France along the Marne River, in north-central France. It must be made from the chardonnay, pinot noir, and/or pinot meunier grape, and by what is known as the *méthode Champenoise*. This is a complicated, expensive, and time-consuming way to engender a secondary fermentation in a bottle of still wine, remove the spent yeast of such a fermentation, and cork and age the bottle for a number of months—even years.

Worth the trouble? I think so, and the whole world seems to agree. That's why more and more countries are forbidding any wines that do not fulfill those requirements to be labeled "Champagne."

(In the United States "champagnes" can be made from grapes other than those mentioned and by other methods—by the Charmat, or bulk, method in a pressurized tank; by transfer, which means from one bottle to another; and even by artificial carbonation. The label on the bottle must tell you—and tell you where the wine comes from, as well—California, New York, Ohio, or wherever.)

The words "Fermented in *This* Bottle" are reserved for the wine made by the true Champagne process—it comes to you in the very same bottle in which it began. The words "Fermented in *the* Bottle" means a wine that starts out like Champagne but is then transferred to a pressurized tank, cleaned of its impurities, and rebottled in *another* bottle.

Champagnes vary in sweetness and body, or *style*. *Brut* means very dry; *extra sec*, dry; *sec*, slightly sweet; *demi-sec*, sweet; *doux*, very sweet. The *style* depends on the house—Taittinger is about as light as they come, Krug and Bollinger about as heavy.

There are also dozens of other French sparkling wines, *vins mousseux* they are called, made of other grapes and some in other ways, but none may use the word "Champagne."

Et Cetera

There are zillions of other wines made all over France—in the Jura, in Provence, in Languedoc, in Cahors, and on and on. Many are eminently worth exploring—for new finds, new experiences, at little cost. Most are not A.O.C. wines, but many are V.D.Q.S. wines (Vins Delimités de Qualité Supérieure), the second rung. The vast majority would be simple *vins de table* or *vins ordinaires*, fine for everyday quaffing.

ITALY

Italy makes an enormous quantity of wine, mostly for home consumption, but lately, more and more for export. According to some, all Italy is a vineyard, from Alps to the bottom of the boot.

The best wines come from the cooler regions in the north—Lombardy, Piedmont, Tuscany, and Veneto. Chianti, Italy's best-known wine, comes from Tuscany. It no longer comes in that straw-covered "fiasco," but is shipped in regular Bordeaux-type bottles. It is marked *"Classico"* if from the original, old vineyards and sports a neck label bearing a black rooster. Newer Chianti vineyard areas have labels featuring a little cherub, a bunch of grapes, ancient ruins, etc., to show the section of Chianti and the *consorzio,* or association, that made it. Brunello di Montalcino, not strictly a Chianti, is from an area a little farther south; it is made from a special clone of the sangiovese grape. Some consider it Italy's best wine.

Piedmont, in northwestern Italy, is the country's most prestigious wine-producing area. From here come Barolo, probably Italy's top red wine, with its companions Gattinara, Barbaresco, and some blends called Ghemme. Barberas and Grignolinos are other wines of the area. Gavi is the *ne plus ultra* white.

From Lombardy, in north-central Italy, you can drink splendid red Grumello, Sassella, and Inferno. From Veneto, in the northeast, come the immensely popular white Soave and red Valpolicella and Bardolino.

From Trentino-Alto Adige, also in the north, comes the white Pinot Grigio, which is now becoming very popular.

For other splendid whites, turn to the Marches, in east-central Italy for famous Verdicchio dei Castelli di Jesi; to Umbria, in the west, for Orvieto, both dry and *abbocatto,* or semisweet; and to Sicily, in the south, for Corvo. Marsala, also from Sicily, is a cooked and fortified dessert wine, so popular in cookery that people forget it is a fine apéritif.

Asti Spumanti, from Piedmont, and sparkling wines from a few other areas are Italy's bubblies. Today, a number are produced by the Champagne process and are being made less sweet than formerly.

SPAIN

There is more arable land in Spain devoted to the grape than in any other country of Europe—but not more wine produced, however. Italy holds that honor.

Sherry is Spain's major contribution to the liquid joys. Sweet, semisweet, dry—known, in that order, as *oloroso* or *amaroso, amontillado,* and *fino*—these fortified wines of Spain are known the world over. Her table wines—Rioja particularly, from north-central Spain— are rapidly gaining a just recognition, as are a number of other wines, still and sparkling, from Panadés, near Barcelona in the northeast. Vega Sicilia, from Valladolid in central Spain, is Spain's most expensive, and possibly finest, table wine.

PORTUGAL

The rosés of Portugal—brands like Mateus and Lancers—have captured America's heart as easy-drinkin', easy-buyin', uncomplicated wines. But do seek out Portugal's crisp white Vinho Verde and rich, red Dão (about 19–22 percent alcohol).

But it is to Portugal we turn for the fortified wine that some say made the British Empire—port, which derives its name from the city of Oporto, in northern Portugal, at the mouth of the Douro River. Made in Portugal mostly by English firms, it is still an "English" wine and it is in England that it is most appreciated and consumed.

Port comes in four general categories: (1) ruby, young and fresh; (2) tawny, older and matured; (3) crusted, a blend of older ports; and (4) vintage, special ports of exceptional years (recent ones are 1963, 1966, 1967, 1970, and 1972).

GERMANY

Hock is the name, derived from Hochheimer wine, given by the British to Rhine wines in general. Those and the German wines from the Mosel valley—in wine contexts called "Moselles"—are now favorites the world over.

Most German wines are, or were, made from the riesling grape, though the hybrids müller-thurgau, ruländer, gutedel, and many others are being grown and used more and more. Sylvaner and gewürztraminer grapes are also seen. Most all of Germany's wines are white and most have an overtone of sweetness. It's the nature of the wine.

Germany has recently propounded new wine rules and classifications. Most German wine is ordinary *Tafelwein,* or table wine, and the new *Landwein,* or regional wines. But as we mount the scale of quality, the next stop is *Qualitätswein,* or wine of quality. The vastly popular blend Liebfraumilch is a *Qualitätswein.*

At the top is *Qualitätswein mit Prädikat* (with special attributes). These are the lords of the realm. They are characterized by increasing degrees of sweetness, from *Spätlese* (late-picked) to *Auslese* (late-picked with a touch of *Edelfäule,* or noble rot, the late-season disease of the skin of the grape, *botrytis cinerea,* that cracks it a little and permits a bit of air to remove some of the moisture and turn the pulp to a raisinlike sweetness). Beyond *Auslese* come the final two degrees of ineffable greatness—*Beerenauslese,* from especially ripe bunches, and *Trockenbeerenauslese,* from grapes selected one by one from the completely affected bunches. Vastly expensive, the latter is an experience in wine drinking everyone should have; only a glass of one of France's greatest Sauternes—perhaps Château d'Yquem—could match it!

OTHER COUNTRIES

Switzerland: Aigle de Murailles, a dry white wine, is my favorite. There is also Fendant, somewhat sweeter, and Neuchâtel. The red wine is predominantly Dôle. Swiss wines are scarce in the United States and often tend to be price-y.

Austria: Austria follows German methods and nomenclature. I like Neuberger (white), Blauburgunder (red), Gumpoldskirchen, and any of the innumerable wines labeled Grüner Veltliner, named for Austria's top grape. Austrian wines are similar to German in taste and nomenclature.

Hungary: Nearly everyone has heard of storied Tokay (Tokaji). Aszú is a sweet Tokay, Szamorodni a dry one. Tokaji Eszencia is today almost legendary. It was the most expensive wine in the world in Emperor Franz Josef's day. He gave Queen Victoria a bottle for every year of her life, on each succeeding birthday! (How could he know she would live to be eighty-two?) 'Tis said he paid twelve dollars each. Such wines are not for the likes of us, but we can afford white Badacsony from the Lake Balaton region, Debrö from south of the Matra range, and the popular red Bikaver, or Bull's Blood, of Eger.

Et cetera: Other wines worth seeking and assaying are Greek St. Helena and Mavrodaphne, Cypriote Commandaria, Jugoslav Dingac, and Turkish Buzbag. The Premiat wines of Romania (Tarnave Castle riesling is splendid) and Trakia wines of Bulgaria (the merlot is a great prize winner) are worth trying—and the prices arc right!

Australia is a large producer of European-style wines that are becoming more and more prominent on the international scene. One may say the same about Canada. New Zealand makes good wine. Chile's wines are first-rate, as are much of Argentina's vast production.

Have fun. Be adventurous. Perhaps you'll be the first on your block to serve a wine from Luxembourg or Uruguay!

A FEW FURTHER TIPS ON WINE

Storage

Unless you have cellar space or a spare room in an apartment, there's no point in buying quantities of wine since you'll not be able to store it as it should be stored. The ideal temperature for storing wine is from 50 to 55 degrees Fahrenheit.

For most of us, that isn't possible, but fear not—wine isn't all that temperamental nor delicate. It can exist for a fairly long spell under less than ideal conditions if (1) you don't roll the bottles around too much in hot summers and (2) keep them on their sides (or even upright on their corks) so that the corks stay wet and hence swollen tight in the bottle. Air is the enemy of wine.

Opened Bottles

Once opened, wine can be kept satisfactorily for a few days at least, if you recork the bottle and keep it in the refrigerator. If you have one or two or more half-empties of the same wine, pour the remainders together so that the air space above the wine is as small as possible.

Temperature

An hour in the fridge is enough for whites. For reds, American homes are pretty warm—five or ten minutes in the fridge instead of in a 70-degree dining room won't do a bit of harm to a red wine. As I mentioned before, the lesser reds can stand a bit of chilling.

Opening Ahead

This is rarely necessary for whites.

For the average red, one half to one hour is fine; more time is needed for the heady, tannic Italians and other full-bodied reds.

Find out for yourself: Open a bottle of red, pour some out in a glass, sip. Now let the rest stay in the glass for half an hour or an hour. Sip again. See if you don't note an improvement.

Glasses

The right glasses are important to your enjoyment of wine. They don't have to be fearsomely expensive crystal (though that's nice)— just be sure they are ample in size (the eight-ounce size is good for white wine, nine-ounce for red) because you should only fill 'em half way up. Leave the top of the glass empty to capture the bouquet.

Oh! yes—choose glasses of clear glass, to reveal the wine's color, and, for heaven's sake, avoid those flat, shallow so-called champagne glasses; use thin, graceful flutes.

VINTAGE CHART

Wine		1981	1980	1979	1978	1977	1976	1975	1974	1973	1972	1971	1970	1969	1968	1967	1966
FRANCE	Bordeaux red	16	15	17	18	15	16	19	15	14	12	18	19	10	8	16	19
	white	17	17	15	17	15	17	19	17	11	13	19	18	15	2	18	13
	Burgundy red	12	14	15	18	14	19	11	15	14	17	19	17	18	6	16	16
	white	14	15	16	17	14	19	13	14	13	15	17	17	18	5	18	16
	Rhone	16	17	16	20	15	18	14	16	16	18	16	18	18	7	16	17
GERMANY	Rhine/Mosel	17	12	16	13	12	20	18	14	17	12	20	16	17	9	17	16
ITALY	Piedmont (Barolo)	18	15	16	20	11	11	10	18	12	6	19	17	14	14	16	7
	Tuscany (Chianti)	18	15	16	17	18	12	18	18	13	10	20	18	17	18	17	13
U.S.A.	California	16/17	17	17	17	16	16	17	18	15	13	18	18	17			

Read above numbers this way: Under 10 - awful
10–14 - mediocre
15–16 - fair
16–18 - good
18–20 - super

Don't make a religion of vintage, though it is something to consider. Remember, there's always some decent wine made in poor years and–though far less likely–some klinkers in good years.

California's climate is more uniform than Europe's, and vintage becomes a mite less important.

Note: 1982–still early, but will probably be superb (18/19) and very large in quantity as well.

TRADITIONAL AFFINITIES
BETWEEN FOOD AND WINE

These are suggestions, not rules. Most people like the combinations listed, but your personal preference should make the decision. Restaurateurs and people who entertain large groups find it best to adhere to the traditional affinities, rather than to experiment. They can be sure that time-tested combinations of food and wine will please nearly everybody.

Champagne is congenial with food both at the start and finish of a meal. As an appetizer, serve *brut;* serve *brut* or *extra sec* up to dessert; serve *extra sec* or sweeter Champagnes only as dessert wines.

Food	*U.S. Wines*	*Imported Wines*
Appetizers, snacks, hors d'oeuvre	Dry sherry, rosé Chardonnay Sauvignon blanc Eastern hybrids: vidal blanc, seyval blanc	Dry sherry, dry Madeira Rosé Chablis Muscadet Rhine and Moselle wines Dry Italian white Italian vermouth, iced
Oysters on the half shell		Chablis, Muscadet
Soup	Medium sherry	Medium sherry Madeira (not too sweet)
Shellfish, fish dishes, cold chicken, and turkey	Johannisberg riesling Pinot blanc Chardonnay Sauvignon blanc French-American hybrid whites: vidal, seyval, ravat	Chablis and other white Burgundy: Meursault Montrachet Pouilly-Fuissé Muscadet Graves Entre-Deux-Mers Rhine and Moselle wines Austrian wine Dry Italian white Alsatian wine
Salmon	Dry white Rosé	Dry white Rosé Beaujolais

Food	U.S. Wines	Imported Wines
Roasts and chops (except pork and veal), pot roasts, liver	Cabernet sauvignon, zinfandel, other light reds	Red Bordeaux Red Burgundy Barolo Barbera
Veal roasts and chops	Dry white	Dry white
Pork roasts and chops	Dry white Rosé	Dry white Rosé Champagne
Roast ham	Rosé	Rosé
Full-flavored red meats, all game, including venison and duck	Pinot noir Gamay Burgundy Cabernet sauvignon	Red Bordeaux Red Burgundy Red Rhone wine Chianti Barolo Barbera
Salad Bowls	Riesling and other light dry whites	Alsatian Dry Rhine and Moselle wines
Nuts	All the robust reds suggested for meat and game Port Sweeter sherry	All the robust reds suggested for meat and game Port Sweeter sherry
Fresh cheeses: farmer, cream, cottage	Rosé	Rosé
Soft cheeses: Brie, Camembert, etc.	Cabernet sauvignon Pinot noir Zinfandel	Red Bordeaux Red Burgundy
Double and triple crêmes	Riesling Sauvignon blanc	Graves Rhine Moselle Alsatian
Hard cheeses: Cheddar, Edam, Cheshire, etc.	Any dry red or white wine	Any dry red or white wine
Desserts	Chenin blanc California sauterne Late-harvest wines	Sweet Rhine wine Sauternes

Food	*U.S. Wines*	*Imported Wines*
Coffee	Brandy	Cognac
	Liqueur	Liqueur
	Sweet sherry	Sweet sherry
	Port	Madeira
		Port

FOOD TO GO WITH DRINKS

The problem of what food to serve with drinks is easy to solve these days. The markets offer an abundance of wonderful delicacies. There are so many appetizing things that can be made up easily for a cocktail party that no one should ever have to resort to the old potato chip and salted peanut routine. Nor should anyone feel compelled to offer the dits and doots popular a few years ago. Trays of tired sections of bread with colored cream cheese are actually not very appealing to most people. My advice is to take it easy. Serve simple, substantial appetizers.

Here are a few of the simplest things to serve with drinks. Most of them can be held in reserve on the shelf or in the refrigerator. Nearly all can be readied quickly when friends and neighbors drop by for drinks.

NUTS

You may buy salted nuts of all kinds in tins. They keep fresh for a long time. The peanut, of course, is the standby, but other varieties are even better and more original as accompaniments to drinks.

Try **Macadamia nuts** from Hawaii with a taste rather like a hot biscuit; **fava beans,** roasted (not really a nut but in the same category); **chick peas,** toasted and salted—very crisp and with a most distinctive flavor; **pistachio nuts**—the large white, salted ones are the best; **walnuts**—these delectable nuts, toasted and salted, are too often neglected; **Mexican sunflower seeds**—crisp and well salted; **giant pecans,** toasted and well salted.

It is no trick to salt your own almonds and filberts and the difference in price is astonishing. Oregon filberts, in particular, are unusual and tasty cocktail bits if treated correctly. Here are a few ideas for preparing nuts that can be eaten warm or stored in glass jars.

Salted Almonds in Their Coats: Spread 1 pound of shelled almonds in their skins in a large, flat baking pan or cookie sheet. Sprinkle with salt to taste and dot lightly with butter. Bake at 350° for 25–35 minutes, or until the nuts are nicely toasted but not charred in flavor. Taste often after the first 25 minutes and be on the alert for the prize moment. Remove the nuts, and let them cool on absorbent paper.

Blanched Almonds: Place the nuts in boiling water for 2–3 minutes to loosen the skins. Slip the skins off with the fingers. Place the blanched almonds in a baking pan or sheet and add 4 tablespoons butter or ⅓ cup oil. Toast in the oven at 350° until nicely browned and crisp. Sprinkle with salt to taste and drain on absorbent paper.

Garlic Almonds: Proceed as in either of the recipes above but add Spice Islands garlic seasoning powder to the nuts before putting them in the oven. Or blend 2 cloves of finely chopped fresh garlic with ⅓ cup oil and pour over the nuts before roasting. Salt to taste when you remove the nuts from the oven.

Curried Almonds: Add 1 tablespoon curry powder to the mixture above and swirl the nuts around in it as they roast.

Chili Almonds: Substitute good chili powder for curry and mix well with the nuts.

Salted Filberts, Pecans, or Peanuts: Place nuts in flat baking pan with salt and butter or oil. Toast at 350° for 25–35 minutes. Drain on absorbent paper.

Garlic or Curry Filberts or Pecans: Place 1 pound nuts in a flat baking pan. Dot with butter and sprinkle with salt. Bake at 350° for 20 minutes or until the nuts are toasted and crisp. Drain on absorbent paper.

DUNKS

The dunk is practically an indoor sport. A bowl of one or two different mixtures with raw vegetables, potato chips or tiny codfish balls enhances almost any sort of gathering. Dunks are made with a mayonnaise or sour cream base, and some have cream cheese or cottage cheese added for body.

HERB DUNKS FOR RAW VEGETABLES (CRUDITÉS)

No. 1—Combine 1½ pints of sour cream with 1 teaspoon salt or more; 1 cup chopped spinach; ½ cup each chopped parsley, chives and dill and 1 clove garlic, chopped fine. Blend thoroughly and let chill for 2 hours before serving.

Mustard: Omit the dill and add 2 tablespoons French mustard and 1 teaspoon dry mustard to the mixture.

Pungent: Omit dill and add ¼ cup chopped green pepper, ½ cup chopped cucumber, and 1 tablespoon chili powder and 1 teaspoon freshly ground black pepper.

Anchovy: Add 1 can anchovy fillets, chopped fine, a hard-boiled egg, chopped fine, and 1 teaspoon orégano. Omit the dill. Add 3 tablespoons capers.

Tart: Add ¼ cup chopped pickled onions and 4 tablespoons capers to the basic mix, omitting the dill. Add 3 tablespoons lemon juice and some freshly ground black pepper.

No. 2—In a blender put 1 package cream cheese, 2 oz. blue cheese, 1 cup sour cream, ¼ cup mayonnaise, ¼ cup chopped parsley, 1 tablespoon ground basil, 1 teaspoon ground thyme. Salt and pepper. Process until smooth.

COTTAGE CHEESE DIP

In a blender place 1 cup cottage cheese, 1 tablespoon Worcestershire sauce, 4 teaspoons chopped onion, 1 teaspoon horseradish, 1 teaspoon caraway seeds, pepper and/or paprika.

VEGETABLES FOR DUNKING (CRUDITÉS)

Any raw vegetable, crisp and cold, goes with these sauces. Some of the less usual ones are tiny *raw asparagus tips* (once tasted they make you wonder why you have eaten only cooked asparagus all these years); the *finger* or *seedless avocado,* now becoming more popular and plentiful; *Chinese water chestnuts,* speared with a toothpick, excellent because of their delightful crispness.

The regulars are *carrots, green onions, cauliflower flowerets, turnips, radishes* (including the *Japanese radish* cut in slices), *zucchini, cucumber fingers, cherry* or *plum tomatoes, celery, anise, fennel,* and *endive stalks.* All very pleasant to munch with cocktails.

DIPS

These are suitable for vegetables but are primarily for seafood.

SHRIMP DIP

Combine 2 cups mayonnaise with ½ cup chili sauce, 1 tablespoon anchovy paste, ½ cup chopped green onions, 2 hard-boiled eggs, chopped rather fine, ¼ cup parsley, chopped fine, salt and pepper to taste.

PLAIN DIP

It's hard to surpass a fine mayonnaise made from good olive oil, egg yolks, salt, pepper, mustard and lemon juice. Perfect with shrimp or lobster or with any fish on toothpicks.

ORIENTAL DIP

Combine 1 cup mayonnaise, 1 cup sour cream, 2 tablespoons chopped ginger, 1 tablespoon soy sauce, 2 tablespoons chopped water chestnuts, 2 cloves of garlic, chopped fine, ½ cup chopped green onions, 1 tablespoon chopped Chinese parsley (cilantro or fresh coriander) if available, ¼ cup chopped parsley. This is elegant with either shrimp or lobster.

SPREADS

This is another easy approach to entertaining. Arrange a big bowl of spread surrounded by thinly sliced and buttered (or not buttered, as you will) rye bread, pumpernickel, lavish in pieces, cracker bread, fine protein bread—any selection of good breads and crackers.

CHEESE SPREADS

Liederkranz, Liptauer, Maroilles, etc., cheeses should be selected carefully. They should be soft but not runny and have a good ripe flavor. Mash them with a fork, adding 2 tablespoons chopped chives,

¼ cup chopped parsley, 3 tablespoons capers, 1 teaspoon dry mustard, 1 tablespoon Worcestershire sauce, and about ¼ cup sour cream. Beat well, taste for seasoning and let the mixture ripen for an hour or two before serving. Sprinkle with paprika and chopped parsley before serving. If the spread seems thin, fold in a little cream cheese to give it body. Many people, in place of making a spread, use Boursin, Boursault, and other spicy cheeses just as they come.

CRABMEAT SPREAD

Combine 1 pound or 2 cans crabmeat with 1 seeded and shredded cucumber, ¼ cup chopped parsley, ¼ cup chopped green onions, and ½ cup mayonnaise. Season with lemon juice and ¼ cup of rum. Let stand 2 hours and drain. Arrange in a bowl and sprinkle with chopped parsley.

AVOCADO SPREAD OR POOR MAN'S BUTTER

Mash 3 very ripe avocados and add ½ cup chopped green onions, 1 teaspoon salt, 1 teaspoon chili powder, and 2 tablespoons chili sauce. Blend well by hand or in the electric mixer. Sprinkle lavishly with chopped parsley. Good as a spread with toasted tortillas or with carnitas.

RAW MEAT SPREAD

This is an all-time favorite with drinks. Combine 1½ pounds ground round steak with no fat (have it freshly ground), 1 egg, 1 teaspoon dry mustard, 1 tablespoon French mustard, 2 tablespoons steak sauce, ½ cup chopped green onions, 1 clove garlic, cut fine. Blend well and place in a large bowl and sprinkle with chopped green onions and parsley. Serve with generous amounts of pumpernickel and hot toast.

ROQUEFORT CHEESE SPREAD

Combine 1 pound Roquefort cheese with ½ pound cream cheese, ¼ pound butter, 1 teaspoon freshly ground black pepper, 1 teaspoon dry mustard, 3 tablespoons Worcestershire sauce, and ¼ cup cognac. Beat well until the mixture is well blended. Refrigerate in small jars. This is an excellent cheese course at dinner.

HELEN BROWN'S IN-A-MINUTE CHEESE SPREAD

This is based on a cheese mixture called Whiz, which is to be found almost everywhere. Combine it with steak sauce, Worcestershire, mustard, chili powder or sauce, or with chopped green onions and salt and pepper. Serve with crackers or pumpernickel. Easy, good and very quick.

CHEESE BALLS

Combine 1 pound cream cheese with 1 pound cottage cheese, 2 tablespoons each chopped green onions and parsley and 1 cup chopped nuts. Season with salt and pepper and dry mustard. Form into small balls, roll in chopped parsley or chopped nuts, and chill for a half hour or so. Serve impaled on toothpicks.

HOT PARMESAN DELIGHTS

This recipe was perfected by the food consultant to the Taylor Wine Company, in Hammondsport, New York. It is simple and tasty.

Combine 1 cup mayonnaise, ½ cup grated Parmesan cheese, 2 teaspoons Worcestershire sauce, dash of onion seasoning or 1 tablespoon chopped green onions. Add 1½ tablespoons sherry or cognac and blend well. Spread on toast squares or on crackers, and sprinkle with a little additional cheese. Brown under the broiler and serve very hot.

APPETIZERS

Sausage Balls (makes about 50)

This is a popular recipe, especially down South.

In a large mixing bowl put 1 pound pork breakfast sausage meat, 1½ cups grated cheddar cheese, 1½ cups flour, 1 teaspoon salt, ½ teaspoon pepper. Work well together. Roll out little marbles (¾″) with your floured hands. Spread balls on a cookie sheet. Put in your freezer compartment until frozen solid. Transfer to plastic bags and leave in freezer until needed. Then bake as many as you wish (3 a person is average) in a 350° oven for 25 minutes. Let cool and stand 10 minutes to crisp. Serve on toothpicks.

Cheese "Things" (makes 3 dozen)

Combine 1¼ cups butter (soft), 2 cups flour, 2 cups grated cheese (cheddar or similar), salt and pepper. Roll into a large sausage, 3″ or so in diameter. Wrap and place in freezer and keep frozen. When ready to use, slice off ⅛″ thick slices. Put on cookie sheets. Bake about 15 minutes at 375°.

Quiche Lorraine (serves 6–8)

In a mixing bowl, work 1½ cups flour, ½ teaspoon salt, ¼ pound soft butter, 2½ tablespoons water. Make into ball. Chill for an hour. Roll dough out thin and line 10″ pie plate or quiche tin. Refrigerate. Cook 1 dozen strips bacon. Drain. Crumble into pie-crust. Preheat oven to 400°. Break 4 eggs into bowl. Add 1½ cups cream, salt and pepper to taste, a pinch nutmeg and a pinch sugar. Mix well. Hold.

Sprinkle 1 cup grated cheese (¾ Swiss and ¼ Parmesan is best combination) over bacon in crust. Pour in the egg-cream custard. Bake quiche 10 minutes. Then reduce heat to 350° and bake another 20 minutes, or until quiche is nicely browned.

(A variation is to add a cup of red onion, diced and sautéed in butter. Pour over bacon before you add cheese and custard. Some use just the onion and eliminate the cheese.)

PIE, PIZZA, OMELET, AND PASTA

Cheese Pie (serves 6)

Crust: 1 package cream cheese
3 oz. soft butter
2 tablespoons flour

Blend cream cheese with softened butter. Add flour. Knead and refrigerate overnight. Next day preheat oven to 375°. Roll out dough to make crust. Shape into buttered pie pan.

Filling: Milk
½ lb. grated Swiss cheese
Salt, pepper, nutmeg

Brush dough with milk. Fill with cheese mixed with salt, pepper, and nutmeg. Bake 30 minutes or until nicely browned.

Pizza (serves 12)

(Warning: It's easier to buy 'em but not so much fun.)

1 package yeast
2 cups flour
1 teaspoon salt
3 tablespoons soft butter

Dissolve yeast in warm water. Mix with other ingredients and knead for 10 minutes. Make a ball. Let stand in warm spot.

Paste: 3 onions, sliced
           3 tablespoons olive oil
           1½ 6-oz. cans tomato paste
           ½ teaspoon oregano
           Salt
           Crushed chili pepper or ½ cup frozen green pepper
           2½ cups water
           2 small cans anchovies, diced

Sauté onion in oil until brown. Stir in tomato paste and seasonings. Add water. Simmer ½ hour. Add anchovies.

Cheese: ¾ cup freshly grated Parmesan, Romano,
             Pecorino, or any combination

Preheat oven to 400°. Get out your pizza pan or pie plate (12-inch or larger). Grease. Roll out dough ¼ inch thick and line pan. Rub dough with olive oil. Pour in paste. Sprinkle with cheese. Bake 25–30 minutes until brown.

Indies Omelet (serves 4)

Make a basic omelet: Beat 4 eggs, 3 teaspoons water, salt, and pepper. Put in well-buttered pan and start to cook. When bottom is firming, add a few slices of almost crisp bacon; a small onion, sliced and lightly sautéed; a few bits of bell pepper and tomato. Fold over omelet. Meantime, heat 3 tablespoons dark or golden rum. Ignite and pour flaming over omelet. Cut and serve. (Four eggs is about the limit for an omelet—at most, 6. For more people, make more omelets.)

Scotch Pasta (serves 6–8)

           ½ lb. rigatoni or macaroni
           3½ tablespoons butter
           2 shallots, chopped
           ¼ lb. smoked salmon, chopped
           2 tablespoons lemon juice
           1 cup heavy cream
           4½ oz. Scotch whisky
           Salt and pepper to taste

Cook pasta *al dente*. In a pot, melt butter and add shallots. Cook 1 minute. Add salmon. Cook 2 minutes. Add lemon juice and Scotch. Cook a few more minutes. Add salt and pepper. Add well-drained pasta.

PÂTÉS

These can be used for cocktail snacks or sandwiches.

HOME-STYLE PÂTÉ

Purchase 1½ pounds lamb's liver, in thin slices, or pork liver; also 1½ pounds ground pork and 1 pound salt pork, cut in thin slices. A good addition is a pound of pork loin cut in paper-thin slices.

Hard boil 4 eggs. Then poach the liver in a skillet with 1 cup wine —red wine or sherry—1 bay leaf, 1 teaspoon salt, 2 teaspoons freshly ground black pepper, 2 cloves garlic. Let it cook slowly, and if there is not enough wine to cover add a little consommé or stock. When the liver is very soft pull it apart and chop it rather coarse. Combine with the ground pork, 1 teaspoon thyme, 3 garlic cloves, chopped fine, 1 teaspoon dry mustard, ½ cup sherry or cognac or whiskey and enough of the broth from the liver to make a fine paste.

Line a casserole or loaf tin with slices of salt pork. Then put down a layer of the meat mixture. Imbed the peeled, hard-boiled eggs in the meat. Sprinkle with chopped green onions and parsley, add a little cognac or whiskey, then cover with meat mixture. Next make a layer of thinly sliced pieces of pork, sprinkle with chopped green onions and parsley, add a little more cognac or whiskey and some freshly ground black pepper. Cover again with the mixture and then salt pork slices. Bake covered for 2½ hours at 325°. Take from the oven, remove cover and place a weight on the pâté to cool. When it is cool, remove the weight and store the pâté in refrigerator till ready to use. Slice very thin.

Serve with hot buttered toast, pumpernickel or hot French bread.

QUICK PÂTÉ

Combine 1 pound good liverwurst, ½ pound cream cheese, ½ cup raw mushrooms, chopped fine, 1 garlic clove crushed and chopped and ¼ cup cognac or whiskey. Beat well together, form into a loaf and serve with toast and buttered thin slices of bread.

BREAD AND SANDWICHES

HOT HERBED BREAD

Split loaves of French bread the long way. Spread with a mixture of ½ cup each chopped green onions, parsley butter with 1 teaspoon salt, 1 teaspoon freshly ground black pepper, and 1 tablespoon fresh or dried tarragon or 1 teaspoon thyme. Press the two pieces together and heat in a 400° oven for 10 to 15 minutes. Cut in 3–4 inch lengths. Serve piping hot with the butter melted well into the bread and the herbs heated through.

SESAME SEED BREAD

Split loaves of French bread in half the long way. Spread with garlic-flavored butter and sprinkle heavily with sesame seeds. Heat in a 400° oven for 10 minutes and brown under the broiler for 3–4 minutes. Cut in 3–4 inch chunks.

CHEESE AND HERB SANDWICH

Split loaves of French bread in halves the long way. Make a paste of ½ pound butter, ½ pound grated Switzerland Swiss cheese, ½ cup chopped green onions, ½ cup chopped parsley. Spread the halves with this mixture and press them together. Heat in a 400° oven for 12–15 minutes or until cheese and butter are melted.

HOT AND PUNGENT CHEESE SANDWICH

Combine ½ pound grated Switzerland Swiss cheese with 1 teaspoon dry mustard, 1 tablespoon curry powder, ½ cup chutney and blend well. Spread split loaves of French bread with the mixture and heat at 400° until the mixture is hot and bubbly and the bread crisp.

INDIVIDUAL HERO SANDWICHES

Split small crisp French rolls in halves the long way. Butter them well. On each roll place a few thin slices of tomato, salami, cheese, licked peppers, anchovies, and sliced ripe olives. Press together and cut in halves. These are substantial and excellent for a large party.

THIN SANDWICHES

A well-made sandwich, of thin bread with plenty of butter and filling, is just about the most satisfying cocktail accompaniment.

Use good breads: pumpernickel, rye, thinly sliced white or whole-wheat bread, protein bread. Spread the slices well with unsalted butter and fill lavishly. Cut the crusts from the sandwiches and cut them into fingers—no fancy shapes are necessary. Pack them in foil and store them in the refrigerator for several hours before serving. Or freeze them the week before and thaw just before serving.

Here is a list of fillings that are very successful for cocktail service:

Thin slices of real Virginia ham

Good smoked ham with pungent mustard

Rare roast beef with horseradish butter

Turkey or white meat of chicken with mayonnaise

Thin slices of corned beef or pastrami

Chopped seeded and peeled tomato

Thin slices of cucumber

Thin slices of onion

Thin slices of onion with parsley and mayonnaise

Chopped ripe olives and onions with mayonnaise

Chopped shrimp with curry mayonnaise

Chopped chicken gizzards and hearts with chutney and fresh ginger

Chopped gizzards with mayonnaise and chopped green onion

Chopped chicken liver with egg and onion

Chopped anchovies, hard-boiled eggs, green onions, parsley

Chopped olives, pimentos, nuts, garlic, parsley

Thin slices of salami

Thin slices of smoked salmon with cream cheese and onion

Thin slices of smoked sturgeon

Pâté de foie (tinned) on white bread with plenty of butter

Chopped cucumber, tomato, onion, ripe olive

Thin slices of tongue with hot mustard

SMOKED FISH

The pungence of smoked fish provokes thirst. It's a waste of time to cut up bits of fish and serve them on toast. Rather, serve a platter of various kinds with bread and butter, crackers, a little oil and vinegar, capers, a pepper mill and a pile of thinly sliced onions. Among the favorites are paper-thin slices of pink smoked salmon, marble-like slices of smoked sturgeon, whole smoked whitefish, smoked butterfish. Smoked eel is elegant. Smoked tuna and smoked cod are wonderful.

HERRING WITH SOUR CREAM

Chop 6 or 8 fillets of pickled herring rather coarsely—enough to make 2 cups. Combine with 1 cup each of mayonnaise and heavy sour cream. Season with ¼ cup each chopped dill and chopped shallots or green onions. Provide a ladle and plenty of thin rye bread.

CANNED FISH

No matter where you are, you'll find canned smoked fish on the market. Thinly sliced smoked salmon is available, also smoked sturgeon, smoked cod, smoked shad, smoked tuna, smoked eel, salmon in a solid pack. Most come in various sizes. I recommend keeping a stock of canned fish on hand for those occasions when you want to offer a snack and drinks.

Sardines of various kinds, served in the can accompanied by toast and crackers, are another favorite cocktail standby.

A rarity, but worth searching for—brood eels (unborn eels) in olive oil. Just heat with a clove of garlic. Spoon over toast points. Lovely, once you get over the idea.

FOOD FOR A LARGE PARTY

BAKED HAM

A large ham—Virginia, Tennessee, or Georgia country ham—is delicious with cocktails. Serve a good-sized one, and be sure there's someone who knows how to carve it in thin, thin pieces across the top. Have bits of thinly cut small French bread and a selection of mustards. The flavor of ham helps to make cocktails more delectable, and there is no waste.

ROAST TURKEY

Turkey has the same good qualities that make a ham so pleasant with drinks. There is no waste and it is better to have some good turkey meat left over than a lot of spreads. Serve it with buttered bread and toast and some good pickles and relish and a bowl of raw vegetables and a good dip.

ROAST BEEF

A large roast of rare beef—just warm, not hot—and slabs of well-buttered and thinly sliced bread are unbeatable for a substantial cocktail snack. Be sure the carver slices the beef as thin as possible, and that you provide good mustard and horseradish with sour cream.

THE THING

This simple "thing" will be consumed by the quart. Children like it, and so do grandparents.

Combine various breakfast cereals: bite-size hunks, oatmeal cereal that comes in tiny rings, the crispies and crunchies that have body. To 2 quarts of the cereal add 1 pound small peanuts, a good sprinkling of garlic seasoning powder, a good sprinkling of chili powder. Salt to taste and dot well with butter. Toast at 300°–325° for 45 minutes to an hour. Shake the pan often and mix well with a spoon or fork so that there is an evenness of browning and crisping and mixing in of flavors. Salt and serve. Store in air-tight containers.

ON YOUR SHELVES

Here's a list of things you can keep on hand for times when you want to have a snack with a drink without too much bother:

Ripe olives or green olives; chill and serve or mix them with a little olive oil and garlic.

Stuffed olives

Cheese biscuits: there are some fabulous Dutch cheese crackers made like puff paste. Heat them and serve.

Anchovies in olive oil. Merely open a good-sized tin and serve with crackers or bread. Lemon should be around.

Sardines of all descriptions
Herring tidbits in tins
Smoked oysters
Tiny cocktail sausages
Tiny cocktail shrimp
Parched corn

DISPENSING DRAUGHT BEER*

There is probably no beverage as sensitive to mishandling as draught beer. Yet three simple fundamental principles control the many details involved in the proper dispensing of perfect "brewery fresh" draught beer. These are *proper refrigeration, cleanliness* and *proper pressures.*

Since draught beer is perishable, it must not be exposed to warm temperatures. The retailer must preserve it by providing equipment that will maintain the temperature of the beer in the barrel between 38°–42° F. These temperatures should be maintained throughout the dispensing equipment so that the beer in the glass as it is served to the consumer will be at 38°–42° F. This range of temperature seems to satisfy the majority of tastes and is too small a variation to affect its flavor or quality.

Cleanliness is a most vital consideration. The beer faucets, tubing, hose, coils, taps, and vents, including direct draw systems, must be thoroughly cleaned at regular intervals. Glasses must be immaculate and sparklingly clean. No effort should be spared to keep the bar clean and bright. Odors and appearances that might be disagreeable must be avoided.

Proper pressure in the barrel is very important. To maintain "brewery fresh" taste in the beer, its natural or normal carbonation must be preserved. The dispensing equipment through which the beer flows must have a pressure that corresponds to the normal carbonation of the beer at the temperature of the beer in the barrel. The size and length of the coil in the dispensing equipment will determine the pressure to be used.

With the dispensing equipment properly set up, the retailer is

* Prepared by Anheuser-Busch, Inc.

ready to serve draught beer. To draw beer, hold the glass at an angle close to the lip of the faucet—open the faucet all the way—lower and straighten up the glass as the beer flows into it so that the desired foam is formed—about one-half inch before the glass is full close the faucet all the way. The foam will rise to the top of the glass, completely filling it without overflowing. A desirable glass of draught beer should include about 20 percent foam.

INDEX